africa

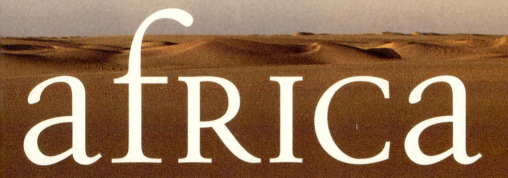

africa

JOHN READER

PHOTOGRAPHS BY MICHAEL S. LEWIS

NATIONAL GEOGRAPHIC

WASHINGTON, D.C.

contents

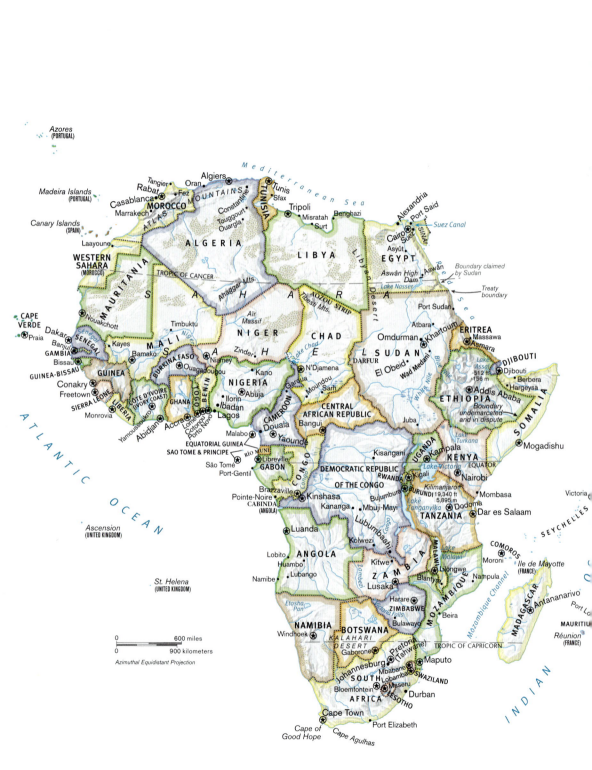

Azores
(PORTUGAL)

Madeira Islands
(PORTUGAL)

Canary Islands
(SPAIN)

Mediterranean Sea

Tangier
Oran
Algiers
Tunis
Rabat
Fez
Casablanca
MOROCCO
Constantine
Marrakech
Touggourt
Ouargla
Tripoli
Misratah
Surt
Benghazi
Alexandria
Port Said

Laayoune

ATLAS MOUNTAINS

Suez Canal
Cairo
Suez
SINAI

WESTERN
SAHARA
(MOROCCO)

ALGERIA

LIBYA

EGYPT

TROPIC OF CANCER

Ahaggar Mts.

Aswân High
Dam
Lake Nasser
Aswân

Boundary claimed
by Sudan

Treaty
boundary

CAPE
VERDE

Nouakchott

MAURITANIA

SAHARA

Tbesti Mts.

AOZOU STRIP

Libyan Desert

Port Sudan

Red Sea

Dakar
Praia

MALI

Timbuktu

NIGER

Air
Massif

CHAD

Atbara
Omdurman
Khartoum

ERITREA
Massawa
Asmara

Banjul
GAMBIA
Bissau
GUINEA-BISSAU

SENEGAL
Kayes
Bamako
BURKINA FASO
Ouagadougou

Zinder

Lake Chad

N'Djamena

SUDAN
DARFUR
El Obeid
Wad Medani

DJIBOUTI
Djibouti
Berbera
Hargeysa

Conakry
Freetown

GUINEA

Kano

NIGERIA
Abuja
Ilorin
Ibadan

Garoua
Moundou
Sarh

CENTRAL
AFRICAN REPUBLIC

Juba

Addis Ababa
ETHIOPIA

Boundary
undemarcated
and in dispute

SIERRA LEONE
Monrovia
LIBERIA
CÔTE D'IVOIRE
(IVORY COAST)
Yamoussoukro
Abidjan
GHANA
Accra
TOGO
BENIN
Lomé
Cotonou
Porto-Novo

Lagos
Malabo
CAMEROON
Douala
Yaoundé

Bangui

Kisangani

Lake
Turkana

SOMALIA
Mogadishu

EQUATORIAL GUINEA
SAO TOME & PRINCIPE
São Tomé
Rio Muni
Libreville
Port-Gentil

GABON

DEMOCRATIC REPUBLIC
OF THE CONGO

UGANDA
Kampala
Lake Victoria

KENYA
Nairobi

EQUATOR

RWANDA
Kigali
BURUNDI
Bujumbura
Kilimanjaro 19,340 ft
5,895 m

Mombasa

Victoria

SEYCHELLES

Brazzaville
Pointe-Noire
CABINDA
(ANGOLA)

Kinshasa
Kananga
Mbuji-Mayi

Lake
Tanganyika

TANZANIA
Dodoma
Dar es Salaam

Luanda

Lubumbashi
Kolwezi

COMOROS
Moroni

Ile de Mayotte
(FRANCE)

Ascension
(UNITED KINGDOM)

Lobito
Huambo
Lubango
ANGOLA
Namibe

Kitwe
ZAMBIA
Lusaka

MALAWI
Lake
Malawi
Lilongwe
Blantyre

Nampula

MADAGASCAR
Antananarivo

Port L

MAURITIU

St. Helena
(UNITED KINGDOM)

Zambezi

ZIMBABWE
Harare
Victoria Falls
Bulawayo

Beira

MOZAMBIQUE

Mozambique Channel

Réunion
(FRANCE)

Etosha
Pan

NAMIBIA
Windhoek

BOTSWANA
KALAHARI
DESERT
Gaborone

TROPIC OF CAPRICORN

Pretoria
(Tshwane)

Maputo

INDIAN

0   600 miles
0   900 kilometers

Azimuthal Equidistant Projection

Johannesburg
Mbabane
Lobamba
SWAZILAND
Maseru
LESOTHO

SOUTH
AFRICA
Bloemfontein

Durban

Cape Town
Cape of
Good Hope
Cape Agulhas
Port Elizabeth

ATLANTIC OCEAN

Senegal
Niger

We all belong to Africa. It is the birthplace of humanity, the nursery where we learned to walk, to talk, to play, to love. Our everyday life is founded upon a talent for innovation that was first used to make stone tools in East Africa nearly three million years ago. From those beginnings we have colonized the globe, built modern civilizations, and traveled to the moon. The thread that joins us to our African ancestors stretches across thousands of generations, but still tugs at the heartstrings as we marvel at Africa's landscapes, wildlife, and people.

Africa is huge—much larger than most people think. All of the continental United States would fit comfortably within the Sahara alone, leaving room in the rest of the continent for China, India, New Zealand, Argentina, and half of Europe. But size is not everything. Africa is also the oldest and most stable of the continents. Its basic form is nearly as old as Earth itself. Its ancient rocks have been less disturbed by volcanoes or earthquakes than any other large landmass. It holds a treasure house of gold, diamonds, and other jewels, as well as vast quantities of minerals such as iron, copper, chromium, and coal.

Once the center of the mighty supercontinent, Pangaea, Africa remained almost stationary as the other continents drifted to their present positions. The Equator has always spanned some part of the continent during the past several hundred million years, bestowing a belt of tropical warmth that helped to make Africa a hothouse of evolution. Fossil algae in the 3.5-billion-year-old rocks of the Barberton Mountain Land are among the earliest known examples of life on Earth, while the same living algae today feed millions of flamingos on the Rift Valley lakes. African crocodiles are the living relatives of the extinct reptilian dinosaurs whose fossil bones have been found in Niger, Tanzania, Zambia, and Lesotho.

The variety of landscapes in Africa is breathtaking. Lofty mountains rise from sun-bleached savannas. The waters of the Nile and the Niger Rivers lay green braids of vegetation through barren desert. The Great Rift Valley stands alone as a unique geological phenomenon. The Great Lakes of central Africa are some of the largest and deepest in the world. The majestic forests of the Congo Basin are the last refuge of gorillas and chimpanzees. The grasslands of the Sahel are unequaled in their expanse. The isolation of Ethiopia's spectacular mountains has fostered the evolution of unique plants and animals. Coral reefs fringe the tropical coasts.

With such a variety of environments, it is not surprising that Africa is home to the greatest numbers of animals in the world. Even today, when wildlife everywhere is threatened, there are healthy populations of elephant, hippopotamus, giraffe, and rhinoceros in Africa. Vast herds of buffalo, wildebeest and zebra roam the savanna, and predators—lion, leopard, cheetah, wild dog, and hyena—stalk and hunt and scavenge as they have done since time immemorial.

Africa's landscapes and wildlife are fascinating, but our closest affinity is with her people, and it is sad that history conspired to keep Africans and non-Africans apart for so long. Even as late as the 19th century, maps of Africa showed vast areas of the continent as blank spaces, labeled "parts unknown." The interior remained another world, whose inhabitants were assumed to be primitive natives awaiting the benefits of civilization. As a result, Africa has been persistently misunderstood and misused by the rest of the world. Even today, many people are unaware of humanity's debt to Africa.

Africa has become widely known as the "Dark Continent"—a phrase loaded with double meaning. The term does not refer simply to the darkness of Africa's forests, to the blackness of African skin, or even to widespread ignorance concerning the continent. Above all, the label refers to the darkness of humanity. That people have behaved barbarically in Africa is undeniable. But this is not an exclusively African characteristic. As history has shown time and again, the stress of collapsing economies and social unrest can tear the social fabric of any peaceful society apart, burying hopes for the future under the problems of day-to-day existence. But Africa's problems should be of particular concern, for the roots of everything human are anchored in the continent. Africa's tragedies diminish us all.

The human line originated in Africa more than four million years ago. The shape of our bodies, the way we stand and walk, our bare skin, and the scope of our minds are all evolutionary adaptations to the African environment. Modern humans existed nowhere else until about 100,000 years ago, when some left the continent via the isthmus of Suez. Though few in number, their descendants eventually colonized every inhabitable niche on the planet.

The drive for prosperity that dominates world history, with its succession of kings, empires, and wars, has little relevance in Africa. The history of humanity's cradleland has been a succession of struggles against a hostile environment. Poor soils, fickle climates, insect pests, parasites, and diseases unique to Africa worked against rapid population growth. While civilizations rose and fell around the world, most African communities stayed just large enough to tend the crops and manage the livestock they needed to feed themselves. Some regions were densely populated at times, and a few kingdoms and empires did develop, but they were exceptions. Even today, when it is often said that Africa's population growth is out of control, the continent supports less than one-quarter the number living on equivalent acreage outside Africa. Compared with other parts of the world, Africa is underpopulated.

The influence of environment can also be seen in the continent's conservative social and political systems. The communities that endured were those that directed their energies toward minimizing failure rather than maximizing returns. Societies grew reluctant to take the risks that development often requires. Knowledge of the past was all-important, and thus gerontocracy, or rule by the elderly, became Africa's defining political system.

Demographers have estimated that by the end of the 15th century, about 47 million people were living in Africa. Though the population should have reached 100 million by 1850, nearly 50 million Africans were lost to foreign exploitation. While Berbers and Arabs traded across the Sahara, the Portuguese sailed down the Atlantic coast, soon followed by Europe's other seafaring nations. Gold was the commodity the invaders sought initially, but before long they were taking slaves as well. Eighteen million slaves left Africa between 1500 and 1850; researchers estimate that for every nine slaves that crossed the Atlantic Ocean, another twelve died. Who knows what Africa might have become without these losses? The slave trade transformed the demographic, economic, and political foundations of the continent.

The slave trade was abolished in the 1800s, but by the end of the century colonial imperialism had replaced it as the main influence on African affairs. The European powers carved up the continent among themselves as they scrambled for Africa's valuable raw materials and mineral resources. Colonial governments assumed control of Africa's destiny. African development came at the whim of foreigners—with paternalistic overtones.

Then, as independence brought Africa a measure of meaningful status on the world stage, the continent became a popular venue for tourists, travel writers, and documentary filmmakers. On safari, in the forests, along the coasts, and on the plains, they portrayed Africa as a surviving remnant of the world at the dawn of humanity. "Dark Continent" imagery still lingered. But the 21st century brings heartening signs of enlightenment.

The African Renaissance movement has stirred the pride and self-confidence of Africa's post-independence generation. And abroad, awareness of humanity's obligation to the continent is growing. There is more to Africa than wildlife and exotic tribal ceremony. Culture seems to set us apart—the Fulani from the Dogon, the farmer from the fisherman, the herder from the company manager, the African from the American—but different cultures are no more than different expressions of a talent we all share: the talent to adapt, innovate, and create. Born in Africa millions of years ago, that shared heritage endows us with a universal sense of humanity. We all belong to Africa.

savanna

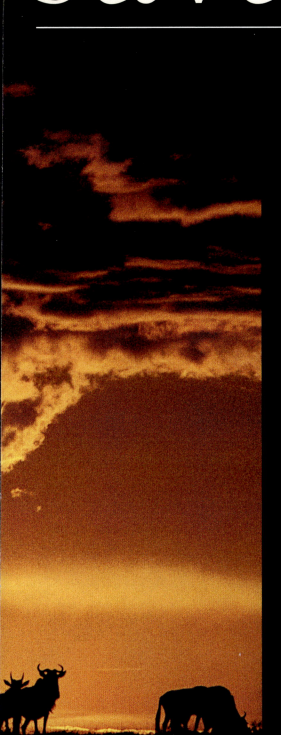

On Africa's golden plains, a miracle of creation sets the stage for the greatest show on Earth. Sunlight, stored as energy in the plants of the savanna, feeds a million wildebeest and zebra, thousands of buffalo, elephant, antelope, and gazelle. Lions lurk in the tall grass, awaiting their chance, and a cheetah races toward its unsuspecting prey like a flash of ancient sunlight.

The scene is timeless. The show has been running for several million years—but never unchanging. Where a giraffe nibbles delicately on acacia treetops in the riverside woodland of a national park, the skyscrapers of Nairobi loom in the background. Here on the plains of Africa, the icons of modern human endeavor rise from the savanna—the place that engineered us.

We learned to be human on the African plains and have taken the talents that Africa gave us to every corner of the world. How this happened—and how we made our debut here—is the great saga of the savanna.

Wildebeest gather at sunset in the Masai Mara Reserve, Kenya. *FOLLOWING PAGES:* Numbering about 350,000, the seminomadic Masai herd cattle across the savannas of Kenya and Tanzania.

the mist has cleared from the valley, drifting downriver on a breeze that sunrise is coaxing from the plains. Trees that minutes ago had been mere shadows in the mist become solid forms. Acacias predominate, each rooted a respectful distance from the other, as though making room. A giraffe appears, browsing daintily on the uppermost branches. Moving elegantly through the woodland in the early morning light, there is an air of peace and stately order in the giraffe's progress.

Antelope and gazelle hardly bother to move aside, zebra merely toss their heads, and the lion keeps its distance from hooves that could crack open its skull. Indeed, the only living things that take exception are the trees, which cannot move out of the way.

The flat-topped acacia trees seem made for the giraffe, and they are, for just as the giraffe's long neck enables it to exploit a food resource that other animals cannot reach, so the uppermost leaves of the acacia are rich in minerals that the giraffe needs for the maintenance of its large bone mass, its powerful heart, and its arterial system. But this is not a passive relationship.

Watch, and we see that the giraffe takes just a few nibbles from each tree before moving on; the acacia has responded to the giraffe's browsing by pumping distasteful tannins into its leaves. As soon as the giraffe finds its breakfast turning sour, it seeks more palatable fare. But browsing also provokes the acacia to emit an ethylene gas that "warns" neighboring trees of an approaching predator. Within minutes, acacias up to 160 feet away have also stepped up their tannin production. And so we find that giraffes browse irregularly, and tend to avoid trees that are downwind.

There is often more to a scene than meets the eye. In the familiar rectangular

The reticulated giraffe is distinguished from its southern cousin, the Masai giraffe, by bolder and less broken markings—an evolutionary result of separation.

map of the world, for instance, Africa appears small in comparison with regions farther from the Equator, but this is a distortion of the Mercator projection. In fact, Africa occupies one-fifth of the Earth's entire land surface. It is also older and less changed by geological events than other parts. Most of the continent has been in place for more than 550 million years, and some of it for as long as 3.6 billion years. Africa was once at the core of a single supercontinent called Pangaea. But even as tectonic forces split Pangaea apart and drove the Americas, Asia, and Australasia to their present positions, Africa hardly moved at all.

Africa's size, age, and stability, combined with its position on the face of the Earth in relation to the sun, have made this continent a unique showcase for the evolution of life itself. Though it would be an exaggeration to say that the most significant developments in evolutionary history occurred first or only in Africa, Africa has been the cradle of many life forms—from the earliest single-cell organisms to the earliest forms of vegetation and the dinosaurs that fed on it, to the first mammals, the first primates, and, most significant of all, the earliest ancestors of our own kind.

More than on any other continent, Africa's geological evolution has been dominated by extension rather than compression. Nowhere is this more true than along the length of the East Africa Rift Valley, which extends more than 2,800 miles from Djibouti on the Red Sea to southern Mozambique. The Rift Valley is currently widening at a rate of up to 0.23 inches per year at its northern end, and will eventually split the continent into two parts. Around 30 million years ago, huge plumes of molten rock rising from the mantle formed a dome on the eastern side of the continent. As the crust of the dome was stretched and thinned, splits developed along lines of weakness. Finally, like an enormous pie crudely pulled apart, segments of the fragile crust dropped into the gaps to create the East Africa Rift Valley—thousands of feet deep, tens of miles wide.

The style and pattern of traditional Masai beadwork identifies the age and status of its wearer.

Volcanic lava spewed up along the edges. In some places it built classic volcanoes like Mount Kenya and Kilimanjaro. Elsewhere the landscape was smothered with lava, which has ultimately broken down to leave those regions endowed with more fertile soils than other parts of Africa. In Ethiopia, for instance, the volume of volcanic rocks extruded is estimated at 84,000 cubic miles, which is enough to cover the entire land surface of North America to a depth of 42 feet. Farther south, 48,000 cubic miles was deposited through the heartlands of Kenya and Tanzania. On the western arm of the Rift, volcanic activity built up the fertile highlands of Rwanda and Burundi and western Uganda. It is no accident that these are Africa's most densely populated regions.

The formation of the East Africa Rift Valley and these mountainous highlands broke up the equatorial and subtropical forests that had previously covered the continent. Meanwhile, the growth of ice sheets over Antarctica fed icy waters into the Benguela Current as it flowed northward along Africa's southwest coast. Cold waters do not generate rain clouds. Southwest Africa became parched, creating the Kalahari and Namib Deserts. At the height of the arid period, the sands of the Kalahari extended all the way to the Congo Basin.

As these cooler, drier conditions reduced Africa's rain forests, the savanna advanced, setting the stage for the greatest show on Earth. Plants and animals evolved, diversified, and multiplied more than ever before or since. There was a huge increase in the number and species of herbivores feeding on the rich new pastures. Inevitably, the number and diversity of predators feeding on the grazers increased too. Though the growth of the savanna virtually eliminated the temperate rain forest flora, the teeming life that the savanna provided in such abundance was an impressive replacement.

Even today, the Serengeti ecosystem alone supports a million wildebeest, 700,000 Thompson's gazelle, 600,000 zebra, tens of thousands of impala, Grant's gazelle, kongoni, topi, eland, dik-dik, bushbuck, waterbuck, giraffe, elephant, rhinoceros, buffalo, and hippopotamus. Among the carnivores are lion, cheetah, leopard, hyena, wild dog, caracal, serval, and jackal. Africa's savannas support up to 200 times more animal life than its forests, which are so often cited as the environment most to be valued.

We might think that only warmth and sufficient rain are responsible for the abundance and diversity on Africa's tropical savannas, but the absence of long cold periods is no less important. In the high latitudes, much evolutionary adaptation has been applied solely to the problems of staying alive through the winter. But on tropical savannas, plant and animal life did not have to evolve ways of surviving months of cold.

It is the sun that keeps things warm, and the shape of the Earth's orbit that gives the tropics such a useful share of its bounty. No animal can live on raw sunlight. But plants can, and they sustain us all. Even the fossil fuels that power our planes and cars owe their origin to the green plants that lived many millions of years ago. The process by which plants capture the sun's energy is photosynthesis, literally "making with light."

The simple equation of photosynthesis—carbon dioxide plus water plus sunlight produces oxygen and sugars—is a metaphor for a complex biochemical process. Cells divide, plants grow, and there is always a residue of sugars in their tissue—the foundation of the food chain. Since grass is concerned only with being grass, most of the energy it absorbs is devoted to keeping itself alive. Only about one-tenth is left to nourish the gazelle that eats the grass, and only about one-tenth of the energy the gazelle gets from the grass nourishes the lion. Available energy diminishes as it moves along the food chain. This explains why there could never be more gazelle meat than grass tissue, and never more lions than gazelles.

The production of the grasslands is immense. During the rains, every square yard of grass on the Serengeti Plain can produce almost two pounds of edible material every month—some 2,850 tons to the square mile. Furthermore, about half of all savanna vegetation can be eaten by some animal or other, compared with less than one-twentieth in a rain forest. So it is not surprising that the Serengeti ecosystem is so densely populated with so many different species. But while the savanna has evolved over millions of years, the relationships between its different elements has not been constant, especially when people have been involved.

For centuries the Serengeti Plain was inhabited by the Masai, nomadic pastoralists whose cattle grazed throughout the region. The grasslands were heavily grazed, and with people cutting wood for their huts and fires and cattle inhibiting the regeneration of trees, the landscape was more open than it is today. Plains game abounded. When an outbreak of rinderpest—a viral cattle disease unknown in Africa before the 1890s—virtually eliminated the Masai as cattle herders, however, vast swathes of the Serengeti rapidly reverted to woodland and plains game populations shrank accordingly. Not until the 1960s, when elephants moved in to avoid hunters in surrounding regions, were the Serengeti woodlands once again opened up to grazing animals.

With the Serengeti now a reserve from which herders and hunters were excluded, wildlife populations increased rapidly. Between 1961 and 1977 the wildebeest population alone rose from 250,000 to 1.5 million. Since every adult female could produce an offspring each year, the population was theoretically capable of doubling in less than three years. But not all offspring survive to maturity. Predators take their toll. Death winnows out the weakest before they reproduce.

Death is fundamental to every living system. Energy and the minerals essential to life could not be recycled without it. If we assume that an individual wildebeest or zebra has an average lifespan of ten years, then it follows that in a population of two million animals, 200,000 will die of old age each year. Add the death of the region's numerous other species, and we can see that death in the Serengeti creates a very large resource.

The hyena is probably the best known scavenger on the African savanna, but the noble lion will not hesitate to dine on the carcass of an animal that died naturally or was killed by other predators. Lions, leopards, cheetahs, wild dogs—virtually all predators will scavenge if they have the chance, though they are not very good at it. In fact, the Serengeti's 7,000 predators miss most of the animals that die from natural causes. The most efficient scavengers in the Serengeti ecosystem are the vultures, which consume more meat than all the mammalian carnivores combined.

Having soared aloft on the columns of warm air that rise from the plain as the day heats up, vultures can spot an animal lying dead on the ground from three miles away, and dive down to it at about forty miles an hour. Their disadvantage is that a diving

Wildebeest cross the Mara River, Kenya. As the seasonal rains move northward from the Serengeti to the Masai Mara, over one million wildebeest follow in their unceasing quest for fresh grazing.

vulture attracts attention. Both lions and hyenas watch for vultures descending, and though we may not find it particularly attractive, this rich and underexploited technique was tailor-made for a distinctive animal that made its first appearance on the savannas of East Africa—our ancestors.

It was of course the upright stance, bipedal gait, and cognitive brain that enabled our ancestors to exploit the resources that other animals had missed. Standing erect on two legs, with the capacity to think about the present and plan for the future on the basis of past experience, humans occupied a unique niche. Small, not especially robust, few in number—fragile figures sharing an ancient landscape with the greatest number and diversity of animals on Earth—they were poised on the first step of a trajectory that would carry their descendants to the stars.

On the southeastern edge of the Serengeti Plain, at a place called Laetoli, archaeologist Mary Leakey and her team swept back a shallow portion of the landscape to reveal a poignant moment in the human story. We walked over what had been a mud pan 3.5 million years ago. In wonder we gazed at a trail of footprints that had been preserved in the delicate fossilized surface. Though very old, the prints were as human as those we leave on wet sandy beaches each summer. Three individuals had crossed the mud pan, one walking in the footsteps of another and a third walking to one side.

As I stood at the head of the trail, with the Serengeti spread below, my mind's eye could see the group walking away from the woodlands that an erupting volcano was dusting with ash. The even depth of each print indicated that their pace had been unhurried. Noting that the prints and stride of one trail were larger than the others, Mary Leakey set aside the rigor of science and wistfully suggested that the prints had been made by a family—a man and a woman walking together with their child. The woman's prints were deeper than might be expected, particularly those of the left foot, suggesting that she was carrying an uneven load—perhaps a baby on her left hip. At one point in the trail the woman appeared to have stopped, paused, and turned to glance back over her shoulder at some threat or irregularity. It was an intensely human reaction that transcended time, Mary said. Millions of years ago, a remote ancestor had experienced a moment of doubt—just as we might today.

Sadiman, the volcano whose ash created the Laetoli fossil beds, is no longer active, but the Laetoli landscape is otherwise not very different from that which existed over three million years ago. The foothills of the highlands are covered in acacia bush, and the upper slopes are swathed in grasses. Westward, the plain extends to a distant horizon, the broad, undulating expanse broken here and there by steep-sided outcrops of granite and gneiss. In shallow valleys, strands of woodland mark the watercourses. Elephants come down from the highlands, giraffes browse on the acacia tops, lions lie concealed in the dun-colored grass, herds of zebra and antelope mingle nervously. Laetoli preserves a sense of Africa in its pristine state, when humanity had but recently learned to walk.

Africa was the cradle of all humanity, and there is little doubt that the population of the savanna was a decisive step in our evolutionary history. All our distinctive characteristics—our ability to walk on two legs for long distances; our hands, with an opposable forefinger and thumb; our bare skin; sweating; and our brain—were adaptations that evolved in response to the demands of the savanna environment. The transition from shuffling ape to striding human ancestor probably occurred as Africa was becoming cooler and drier and its forests were shrinking. As competition for dwindling resources intensified, our ancestors moved out to the savanna, where access to a more widely dispersed food supply prompted the evolution of bipedalism.

But while the edible resources of the savanna can support much more animal life than the forests, there were formidable new constraints. Gathering the widespread resources called for hours of walking in the heat of the sun, which in turn posed the question of water and where to find it. Our human ancestors who crossed the Laetoli mud pan were about the size of a modern eight-year-old. Their water requirements were less than ours, but even they could not have traveled more than seven miles from water as they foraged for food. This is because we sweat to keep cool.

At first, sweating seems a perverse way of keeping cool in a tropical environment where water is often scarce. After all, grazing animals spend their days exposed to the full impact of the tropical sun. They don't sweat, but nor do they have large brains; paradoxically, the large brain and sweating to keep cool are inextricably linked. All mammalian brains are extremely sensitive to temperature, and variations of more than a few degrees can be lethal. The body temperature of animals on the plain often rises above danger levels, but their bodies are able to control the temperature of the blood that travels to their brains.

Our ancestors did not have this capability, but they developed the most effective body-cooling system of any mammal: sweat glands that cover the entire body, naked skin, and an erect stance. Simply by standing upright, our ancestors avoided 60 percent of the solar radiation to which quadrupeds are exposed when the sun is directly overhead. Furthermore, standing erect brought more of the body in contact with breezes and winds, while a naked skin ensured that sweat pores could rapidly transfer body heat to the surrounding air.

Cooled by the most efficient means of any mammal, the brain became larger and more useful as our ancestors foraged more widely on the savanna. While other animals evolved specialized physical attributes to enhance their chances of survival—the giraffe's long neck and the elephant's trunk are classic examples—evolution endowed our ancestors with a highly specialized capacity for thinking. Initially it may have evolved to control the demands of eye-hand coordination, but it was destined to become our main survival tool.

The downside is that brain is expensive tissue, consuming over sixteen percent of the body's energy despite representing

While other antelope and herbivores eat one main food source year round,
the impala changes its diet with the seasons.

only two percent of body weight. Furthermore, it burns up energy nine times faster than the rest of the body and must be continously supplied with fuel. As the human brain evolved, keeping it running was no less demanding than keeping it cool. And so our ancestors learned to seek out high-quality, nutrient-rich foods of which relatively small quantities would suffice—seeds, nuts, tubers, and eggs—along with significant quantities of protein in the form of meat.

Thus, satisfying the demands of a large brain has called for a good deal of cognitive effort on the part of the brain itself. The success of this interactive relationship is self-evident, for it is the foundation of all human behavior and achievement: technology, language, and culture. And all was a consequence of adapting to life on the tropical African savanna.

One Sunday afternoon, some weeks after I had moved to Nairobi in early 1969, I drove out of the city, down the Mombasa road. Where the ribbon of tarmac crossed the Athi Plains, I turned onto a dirt track; soon the track petered out and I continued

The flat-topped acacia, *Acacia tortilis*, is perfectly adapted to Africa's climate. The crowning layer of tiny leaves balances the tree's need for sunlight with the dangers of drying out.

on foot through the low, scrubby vegetation. At one point, where the downpours of a previous wet season had converted the trail into a shallow watercourse, some fragments of stone caught my eye. I knelt and found a small cache of knapped flakes eroding from the banks of the watercourse. At first I thought they were crude arrowheads, but in fact they were small blades that you might hold between thumb and forefinger, and use as a knife.

That I should have found them on a Sunday afternoon stroll did not seem remarkable at the time. After all, I had recently returned from Koobi Fora in northern Kenya, where Richard Leakey and his team were excavating the fossil remains of all manner of creatures. Nonetheless, kneeling on the Athi Plains that afternoon, alone with a scattering of stone blades, was an evocative moment. They could have been made a hundred thousand years ago, when stone tools were the cutting edge of human survival. And now here I was, with the modern city of Nairobi shimmering in the heat haze to the north.

FOLLOWING PAGES: Surprise attacks from the cover of tall grass are more than just play for 14-month-old cheetah cubs. Such behavior teaches young cheetahs the skills of survival on the plains.

From maned lions to bongo antelope, Africa's hunting concessions claim to offer the best sport of its kind. Safaris attract people from around the world to the African savanna—birthplace of evolution.

As a species, we have been alone in the world since the last Neandertals became extinct about 25,000 years ago, free to colonize the globe and exploit the Earth's resources without competition from others of our kind. No other mammals have ever been so widespread and so alone. But it was not always like this. Many new hominid species have emerged, competed, coexisted, and succeeded—or failed—since our ancestors stepped onto the savanna four to five million years ago. Some of them migrated from Africa via the Isthmus of Suez and established populations as far afield as China and Indonesia. Others colonized Europe, and it was from this branch that the Neandertals evolved, remaining relatively common throughout the continent until they became extinct.

Meanwhile, branches of the ancestral tree were growing in Africa, culminating between 150,000 to 200,000 years ago in the appearance of a very distinctive hominid. These newcomers were tall and slender, their chins were jutted forward, their faces were tucked in under the skull, they had a high forehead, and their brains were as large as ours. The connection is unmistakable. These were the first representatives of our species, *Homo sapiens*—wise man.

All the other representatives of the hominid family disappeared not long after this, for reasons we may never fully know. But Africa filled up with people like ourselves, and before long they spilled out of the continent and colonized the rest of the world. Geneticists have estimated that the numbers involved in this second migration were very small, which means all their descendants are very closely related. In fact, a New Yorker and an Australian Aborigine are likely to be genetically closer than two people from the same town in Africa. This is because Africans inherited the genetic characteristics of more ancient and diverse populations, while New Yorkers and Aborigines both inherited the diversity of a species that had only evolved in the relatively recent past.

The geneticists' reports have the authority of science but lack the charm of earlier attempts to explain where we came from. A legend from East Africa, for example, goes like this: As he lay dying, an old man sent each of his three sons out into the world with a gift that would set them up for life. The first received an arrow and went off to make a living by hunting—becoming the Dorobo. The second was given a hoe and learned how to till the land and grow crops—the Kikuyu. The third received a stick and began herding cattle—the Masai.

The legend of the arrow, the hoe, and the stick summarizes the means by which people have exploited the terrestrial resources of Africa: hunting, farming, and herding. The divisions are deeply established and often sustained by distinguishing features of appearance, custom, and, too often, mutual antagonism. But the distinctions are ecological, rooted in the environmental zone each group occupies.

The Masai can no longer range across the plains of the Serengeti, but they still herd their cattle along the full length of the East Africa Rift Valley. To the north of the Serengeti and east of the Mara in Kenya, cool uplands once provided a retreat for the Masai and their cattle in the dry season, when the savanna was parched. On the rising gradient above this dry-season pasture, where the grass glades merge into woodland and forest, Kikuyu farmers cleared the land, built houses and fences, and planted crops that flourished at that altitude. Higher still, on steep slopes where crops would not thrive, the Dorobo took charge, exploiting the resources of the forest. They collected honey and wild fruits, trapped wild animals, and were conversant with the medicinal properties of little-known forest plants.

In good times the Dorobo gathered more forest produce than they needed for themselves. They traded the excess with the farmers, seeking the roots and grains that are scarce in the forest. In turn, the farmers were grateful for a supply of game meat, for that meant not having to slaughter their own animals. Likewise, the Kikuyu farmers traded with the Masai herders, exchanging grain for dairy produce, leather, and young animals. In each case, the need to produce a surplus that could be traded for essentials from a neighboring ecological niche encouraged people to make the most of what they had.

This is, of course, an idealized account. Climate, lack of sufficient numbers, antagonism, and most importantly the events of history have conspired against this Garden of Eden scenario. For one, the Dorobo were not always confined to the forests. Hunters like them had once ranged throughout Africa and retreated to their refuges in the forests and the deserts only as other groups move in and took over their lands. The people of the stick had moved onto the high savanna of southern Kenya by 2,600 years ago, and the people of the arrow may not have been totally averse to their arrival, since domestic stock are easier to kill than wild game. But the more overwhelming incursions came centuries later, with the arrival of the people of the hoe from the west.

The Kikuyu had crossed the savannas and colonized the high southeastern shoulder of Mount Kenya by the beginning of the 17th century. The soils and climate were good, and the Dorobo hunters and gatherers who had previously occupied the region were either absorbed into the Kikuyu population or displaced as Kikuyu pioneers pushed back the forest. The pioneers were generally young men who formed an *mbari*—a pioneer band—to occupy a ridge on the high, forested slopes; then, having worked to clear the forest, they divided the land among themselves.

With their main center at the confluence of the Thika and Thagana Rivers, the Kikuyu mbari pushed on, heading upstream along the course of the Thagana River and west into the valleys of the many tributaries that flow from the Nyandarua Range. Facing east, the Nyandaruas catch the moisture-laden monsoon winds blowing in from the Indian Ocean, and so they are fertile and highly suited to intensive agriculture. Thus the Kikuyu population increased rapidly, spreading more waves of settlers south to present-day Nairobi. During this period of expansion, the Kikuyu developed their symbiotic relationship with the Masai of the savanna. Goods were exchanged, words borrowed, and customs adopted. A good deal of intermarriage took place as well. More than half the Kikuyu in some districts are believed to have Masai blood in their veins.

Much of the vegetation that the pioneering farmers had been obliged to clear from the slopes of the Nyandaruas and Mount Kenya was useful, but one tree, above all others, was revered by the first

Children walk to school in Karatina, many barefoot and from homes without running water or electricity. An educated child is the promise of relief from poverty. But there is no free education in Kenya.

pioneers—the wild fig, *Ficus natalensis*. The mature wild fig is a massive tree, wide in girth, with branches so close together and leaves so densely packed that even a bird or a leopard might get lost in its canopy, they say. The wild fig was never felled—perhaps because of its daunting appearance, perhaps because its sap is sticky and can cause rashes, perhaps because its timber is soft and not useful—or perhaps because its location usually signified the presence of a spring. Whatever the case, the wild fig is revered by the Kikuyu to this day. A huge specimen stands on the slopes of the Nyandaruas, facing Mount Kenya, at Mukurue wa Gathanga. According to Kikuyu tradition, this is the Garden of Eden—their birthplace.

Rested after a bumpy, spine-jolting ride from Nairobi, Alice Wangui walks with her son, Scott, down lanes where she had played as a child. Though she lives in the city, this is the place Alice calls home. Generations of her family have treasured this precious corner of the Kikuyu homeland. Both she and Scott were born here, as were her father and grandfather.

"That is a must," Alice says. "You're supposed to give birth where you were born. It's very important. You are supposed to go back to your home."

alice Wangui is a single mother expecting her second child. A thoroughly modern and successful woman who runs her own hairdressing salon in Nairobi, Alice has access to the best of the city's medical attention. Still, she has decided to have the baby in the village where she herself was born. Her first child, seven-year-old Scott, was born there, and his sister (if the baby is the hoped-for girl) must be born there too, Alice says, in the land of the family's Kikuyu forefathers. Like most Kikuyu, Alice feels a strong attachment to the land of her birth—even though she lives and works so far away.

The Kikuyu are the largest of Kenya's ethnic groups, an eastern outpost of the farming communities that were spreading steadily south and east from the Great Lakes region of central Africa one thousand years ago. By the early 1600s the Kikuyu had settled throughout the highlands of what is now Kenya, with their spiritual homeland firmly established in the beautiful high country of the Nyandarua Range, facing Mount Kenya, where monsoon winds from the Indian Ocean brought ample rains to fertile soils.

Alice's village nestles in the foothills of the Nyandaruas, close to the small market town of Nyeri, but still over 90 miles from Nairobi. The bus journey will be long and uncomfortable—and risky for a woman in the last month of pregnancy. The doctor urges Alice not to make the journey at this late stage, but Alice is determined to go. A baby born in Nairobi comes from nowhere, she says.

Desert

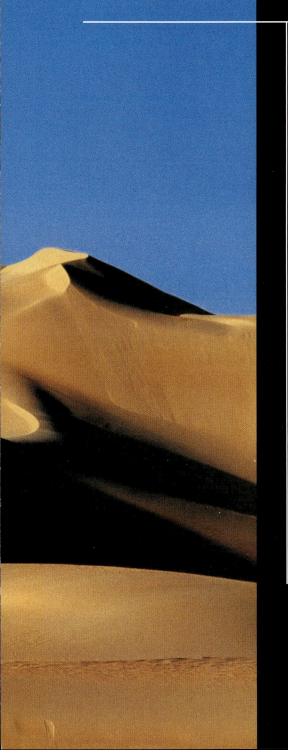

The Sahara is the largest desert on Earth. A wasteland of terrifying beauty, with golden dunes winding sinuously to distant horizons. An environment of contrasts, where the burning sand destroys life and the shady oasis sustains it, where the sun saps moisture from the body by day, and where the cold of deep space freezes the desert at night.

The Sahara is also the Earth's most compelling record of climate change. Fifteen thousand years ago the desert was even drier than it is today. Nine thousand years ago it was a paradise of savannas, lakes, rivers, and woodlands in which Africans first began to plant crops and herd livestock. When the desert dried out again, the pioneers took their newfound talents into the Nile Valley and the distant reaches of Africa.

But evidence of the desert's former generosity remains—in the huge volumes of water that lie under the sands, feeding desert wells and green oases, and in the salt of dried-out lakes that Tuareg camel caravans transport from the desert to the towns.

Dunes of the Sahara rise to heights of nearly 1,000 feet. *FOLLOWING PAGES:* Men have farmed the banks of the Nile for thousands of years, reaping the benefit of both the water and the silt brought down from central Africa.

Desert

as a city boy sent to spend the war years in the countryside of Wales, I was fascinated by the bird life. Sparrows and starlings were the most I could expect at our London home. Yet the garden in Llantwit Vadre thronged with tits and finches, blackbirds, thrushes, and the occasional wagtail. By the time I was eight, I knew all the common birds and quite a few of the rarer ones, but for all my searching I never did see the cuckoo, the herald of spring.

The swallows and swifts arrived in May, nesting under the gables and in the sheds on the farm. In autumn I would watch them gathering in rows on the telephone wires, ready to migrate south. The idea that these small creatures could fly all the way to Africa was almost beyond belief, but I admired their ability to escape the European winter.

I thought of the birds flying away as our birds, but I've since learned that even though they hatch in Europe, many of them actually spend most of the year in Africa. They should perhaps be thought of as Africa's birds, merely gracing the European summer with their presence.

The distances they travel are prodigious, but the trans–Sahara crossing is the most demanding part of the trip: 930 miles on the most direct route and over 1,200 miles on the diagonal trajectory that the birds often follow. Flight times range from 40 to 60 hours and the crossing is made without a stop in most cases, for oases are few and far between.

The total number involved in the migration has been estimated at 2.5 billion birds. Few are seen from the ground, but radar observations have confirmed the passage of thousands flying at altitudes of 9,800 feet and above, where the thin air offers less resistance and energy reserves

Water cascading from the mountains behind Timia, in central Niger,
provides a swimming pool for the Tuareg village children.

last longer. The majority are songbirds weighing little more than the airmail letters we send winging around the world. They in particular must take on a lot of fuel for the trans–Sahara flight. A sedge warbler feeding on the savanna fringes of the desert, for instance, will put on more than half its weight in fat before taking off.

While the savanna has encouraged plants and animals to maximize their potential, the desert has tested their ability to survive. Nowhere on Earth is the living world's dependence on water so clearly demonstrated. Deserts are one of the world's most widespread environments, covering between one-quarter and one-third of the land surface. In Africa alone, 40 percent of the land surface is dry and hot enough to qualify as desert: the Kalahari, the Namib, and the Karoo in southern Africa; the Denakil, Ogaden, and Chalbi in East Africa; and of course the Sahara.

The Sahara is the largest and most awe-inspiring desert on the planet. It covers about 3,500,000 square miles—about 6 percent of the Earth's entire land surface and roughly equal to the size of the United States. From the savannas of northern Mali, Niger, Chad, and Sudan, it stretches 1,200 miles north to the Atlas Mountains and the Libyan coast of the Mediterranean, where Saharan sands blow across the ruins of 2,000-year-old Roman cities. From the Red Sea in the east, the desert spans the continent to the Atlantic Ocean—3,000 miles away.

Its influence does not stop at the coast. Windblown Saharan sands lie in the seabed deposits of the mid-Atlantic, and Sahara dust is carried over great distances to the Caribbean and eastern South America. The Sahara alone accounts for 60 percent of all the sands and dust that are blown into the atmosphere each year—approximately 300 million tons in total.

The Sahara is larger and drier than the rest of the world's deserts. Most of it lies beyond the influence of oceans that modify temperature and humidity. The Sahara consequently has less "weather" than virtually any other place on Earth, receiving an average of over ten hours of sunshine every day throughout the year. In fact, the sun beats down on the Sahara with such force that it could evaporate water to the depth of an eight-story building in the course of a year. Average high temperatures rise well above 104°F in the southern part of the desert and exceed 95°F over wide areas. The world's highest temperature ever recorded was in the Libyan desert: 136.4°F in the shade.

Rain is a rare phenomenon. Monthly or even annual averages are meaningless. It is not uncommon for one place to receive more than the annual average in a single day while another, just a few miles away, remains bone-dry. At the Kharga Oasis in Egypt, children have lived to the age of seven before ever experiencing a fall of rain. But four inches of rain falling over a short period—as is often the case in the Sahara—will produce far more vegetation than the same amount falling in equal portions every week throughout the year. So despite too much sunlight and too little rain, the Sahara supports a surprisingly large number of plant species: 80 of its 1,200 species are not found anywhere else in the world.

The plants of the Sahara are distinguished by their adaptations to the harsh environment. The lichens and algae that are found clinging to desert rocks, for example, shut down their life processes almost completely whenever water is not available, which ensures survival but also means they grow very slowly. Annual flowering plants, on the other hand, grow very fast, producing the swaths of colorful flowers that are so well-known from the Namib Desert and the Karoo. They effectively escape drought by not even attempting to live except when it rains, and then only briefly. Great banks of their seeds may lay dormant in the sand for years. Their trick is to germinate with the first rain, grab available nutrients, mature, and set seed as quickly as possible. The process cannot be stalled or reversed. If the rains fail after the seed has germinated, the young plant will wither and die before it has flowered and set seed.

Perennial desert plants take no such chances. They have adopted a selfish strategy, more concerned with keeping themselves alive than with producing the seed of future generations. They build up reserves whenever times are good, then hunker down to keep life ticking during the bad times that inevitably follow. Extensive root systems are common, and some plants carry the strategy to excess. For example, a shrub, *Leptadenia pyrotechnica*, typically has roots that delve 38 feet underground and extend up to 33 feet all around the plant. Such a root system exploits about 30,014 cubic feet of soil (the volume of a four-bedroom, two-story house)—all for a bush that would not overcrowd a suburban patio.

For all its open horizons, the Sahara has a hidden history. At its heart stand the Tassili-n-Ajjer Mountains, a sandstone massif scoured by the wind into a labyrinth of winding chasms and grotesque sandstone pillars. In this moonscape the days are scorching hot, the nights freezing cold. The wind frays the nerves, and the thread of life itself never seemed so fragile. Yet in a narrow gorge you will find a group of living cypress trees. The trees crown a jumble of rocks and wind-polished boulders, their exposed roots writhing through crevices and beneath tilting boulders as they probe for water. The cypresses regularly produce cones with viable seeds, but none germinate in the gorge. The ground is too dry.

Tree ring analysis has established that the cypresses are between 2,000 and 3,000 years old. When they were saplings, streams ran through the Tassili-n-Ajjer Mountains. The Sahara was then a well-watered savanna with wildlife and lakes and a scattering of people who hunted and fished and kept herds of cattle. They harvested wild sorghum, and from time to time sheltered in the shallow caves of the Tassili-n-Ajjer, where they decorated the smooth sandstone walls with paintings that illustrate their everyday lives.

The Tassili-n-Ajjer caves contain more than 4,000 paintings and many more rock engravings. Experts regard it as one of the world's greatest collections of prehistoric art. The oldest paintings are thought to date back to 6000 B.C. and show wild animals and hunters and masked figures whose sinuous bodies exactly convey the movements of a dance. Herders appear to have entered the gallery around 5000 B.C., rendering bold, colorful pictures of cattle with sweeping horns and swishing tails. From about 1200 B.C., paintings of horses and chariots appear, documenting the time when people from the Mediterranean were in contact with the inhabitants of these central Saharan regions. The urgent activity of these scenes suggests a threat—and indeed, the people were being threatened, but not by invading forces. The environment itself had turned

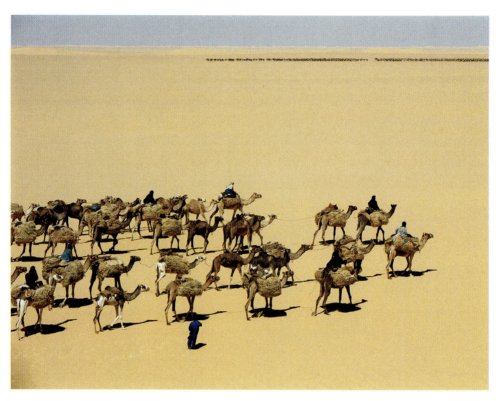

Caravans with thousands of camels once plied the route to Bilma across the Sahara, carrying salt from the desert to the Sahel and forest regions of West Africa.

against them. The remorseless influence of a changing global climate created barren desert wastes.

Like a folk memory lingering on from better times, the name Tassili-n-Ajjer means "plateau of the rivers." No other place on Earth offers such a compelling image of climate change. In a twinkling of geological time a garden became a desert. The sun, which had once nurtured life, evicted all but those with the capacity to adapt. The cypresses hang on in their original form, but one day they, too, will be gone forever.

It would be a mistake to think that this drying up of the Sahara was a unique event.

On the contrary, it had happened before. Seven thousand years ago the Sahara was a landscape of savannas, lakes, and rivers. Yet eight thousand years before that it was even drier than it is today. These oscillations from wet to dry and back again, each spanning thousands of years, have been going on for millions of years.

The verdant green croplands of the Nile Valley are the very antithesis of the bleached Saharan landscape through which the river flows, but these two contrasting features together constituted a primary force in the development of settled human society in Africa. Ancient Egyptian civilizations may

Cairo, seen here across the Nile and the Sixth of October Bridge, is home to ten million people and growing fast. Its expanding population builds on Egypt's already scarce agricultural land.

have refined the practice of extensive agriculture, but their crops—wheat, barley, peas, and lentils—all arrived from the Fertile Crescent of the Near East long after the cultivation of indigenous food crops had begun in what is now arid desert. The first cereal crop—sorghum, which is indigenous to Africa—was planted in the Sahara 8,000 years ago.

And agriculture is not the Sahara's only first. The continent's first pots were fashioned from Saharan clays over 9,000 years ago. And Africa's earliest known domesticated cattle were herded across the savannas of the Sahara more than 6,000 years ago.

In effect, the Sahara acted as a pump, drawing in people from surrounding regions during good times, and driving them out again as conditions deteriorated. In the process, the Sahara's inhabitants applied the human talent for adaptation and innovation to greater effect than elsewhere on the continent.

Like many people, I grew up with the idea that Timbuktu is the most romantic and faraway place imaginable. So it was an agreeable surprise to discover that I could fly there from Mopti, in Mali, where I had been reporting on some archaeological work. As the only visitor in town I soon made the acquaintance of Mohamed Ali, who would leap from the shade of the palms whenever I appeared, insisting that I should ride with him out into the desert. Mohamed was a Tuareg, and his family ran a camel train bringing gravestone-size slabs of salt to Timbuktu from the Sahara mines at Taoudenni, nearly 400 miles away.

The name Tuareg comes from an Arabic term meaning "God forsaken," which is presumably a comment on their objection to the advance of Islam into the central Sahara during the 11th century A.D. But their complaint was more commercial than religious: They objected to the increasing presence of Arab traders in their territories, especially those inspired by the promise of gold.

Gold coins struck in Carthage between A.D. 296 and 311 are probably the first indication of African gold reaching the wider world. The amount of coinage was small to begin with, but the increasing volume of gold circulating in Roman North Africa from the fourth century A.D. indicates a substantial trans–Saharan trade at that time—no other source could have sufficed.

With the Arab conquest of all North Africa by 711 A.D., the demand for West African gold intensified. The trans–Saharan trade was boosted still further when Europe began minting gold coins: at Florence in 1252, in France from 1254, and in England

from 1257. Between the 11th and the 17th centuries, West Africa was the leading supplier of gold to the international economy, and in the late Middle Ages it accounted for almost two-thirds of world production. But the trans–Saharan share dwindled to a trickle toward the end of the 15th century, when the Portuguese outflanked the trade with a sea route to the West African coast. Their caravels landed on the shores of what is now Ghana in 1472, and the trading center they established soon became known as El Mina (the mine), the seaboard as the Gold Coast—the name it bears still.

Gold was plentiful, but the Portuguese had difficulty paying for it. Horses did not live long in the equatorial climate, and there was a limit to the amount of cloth and sundry goods that the Akan people, who controlled the Gold Coast trade, would accept. Firearms were banned as an item of trade by the Pope, who feared they might reach the hostile forces of Islam. Finally, the Portuguese discovered an African commodity that the Akan would readily accept in exchange for their gold, one that was abundantly available: slaves.

The arrival of the Portuguese on the Gold Coast fatefully coincided with the expansion of the Asante (a branch of the Akan) into the forested regions where gold was found. They needed more labor for forest clearance, farming, and mining, and the Portuguese were able to oblige by shipping in slaves from around the Bight of Benin,

Salt evaporation ponds at Fachi, Niger, attest to the transformation of the Sahara from well-watered savanna to desert. Ten thousand years ago this region was a vast lake.

where Benin and Igbo leaders readily handed over people they had captured and were less fussy about the goods received in return. Thus the seaboard adjacent to the Gold Coast acquired the sobriquet by which it is still identified in some reputable atlases—the Slave Coast—and the Portuguese became middlemen in an indigenous slave trade. Between 1500 and 1535 they shipped many thousands of slaves across the Bight of Benin.

They also shipped significant numbers back to Portugal. The first human cargo arrived at Lagos on August 8, 1444, and African slaves were brought to Portugal in such numbers that by the 1550s they made up nearly 10 percent of the Lisbon population. Inevitably, the profits flowing into Portugal from Africa's west coast caught the attention of Europe's other maritime nations, and the Portuguese monopoly was steadily eroded by interlopers who, more

often than not, would hijack Portuguese gold and slave ships on their return voyage. In 1562, English adventurer John Hawkins added another dimension to the trade when he acquired 300 slaves from West Africa, "partly by the sword, and partly by other meanes," and sailed them across the Atlantic to the Caribbean islands, where they were set to work in the recently established sugar plantations.

Hawkins's voyage heralded the moment at which Europe's sweet tooth began to shift the course of history in Africa and the Americas. Sugar was in high demand, and Hawkins bears the dubious distinction of starting the triangle trade in the Atlantic. Goods from Europe were exchanged for slaves in Africa who were exchanged for sugar in the Caribbean, which sold in Europe at a profit that returned the initial investment many times over. Over the next three centuries, more than nine million slaves were shipped across the Atlantic— up to two million of whom perished en route. The largest proportion, 42 percent, were sold to plantation owners on the sugar islands of the Caribbean; 38 percent were shipped to Brazil (by the Portuguese); fewer than 5 percent were landed in what is now the U.S. Large numbers of slaves from West Africa also were transported across the Sahara for sale in North Africa, and yet more were shipped from East Africa to Arabia.

The Tuareg doubtless participated in the slave trade as suppliers, customers, and transporters, but they were also transporting a commodity that helped to sustain life: salt. The Sahara is the greatest repository of salt in Africa. When the lakes and waterways of the wet period began to evaporate, the receding waters leached salts from the soil; the lakes eventually dried out and became salt pans. Several million tons fill a huge lake basin north of Bilma in Niger, and other vast deposits are located at Taoudenni and Teghaza in northern Mali and at Tichit in Mauritania—hundreds of miles from the people who need it and have no other source.

Most people get enough salt from their everyday diet, but our taste for salt encourages us to consume more than we need. Throughout the world, throughout history, salt has been the most widely sought-after food supplement, and wherever salt was not readily available, it became a strong incentive for the development of trade. Indeed, the movement of salt from source to consumer in Africa probably marked the world's first long-distance trade routes. The volume of the salt trade was always impressive, and by the 19th century, when European explorers first succeeded in reaching the fringes of the central Sahara, the

OPPOSITE: **Between one and six million tons of high-quality salt lie in the Bilma Basin. At the height of the Sahara trade, 70,000 camel loads were exported annually.** FOLLOWING PAGES: **With splayed feet and webbed toes, the single-hump camel can carry heavy loads over soft sands that no other transport could cross.**

volume of the trade was vast. An eyewitness account reports that as many as 70,000 camel loads of salt were exported from the Bilma region alone each year.

The Bilma salt traveled due south, supplying primarily the salt-deficient Sahelian regions of Niger, Chad, and northern Nigeria, with significant amounts traded onward from there to people in the forest regions of Cameroon and southeastern Nigeria. Rock salt from deposits in the western Sahara at Tichit, Teghaza, and Taoudenni also traveled south to join routes supplying the Sahel and regions extending from Nigeria to Senegal.

The Niger River was once a major artery of the Saharan salt network. Timbuktu, the fabled city poised where the Niger curves around the ancient gold-laden rock core of West Africa, was the clear-inghouse. Within living memory, tens of thousands of camels congregated at Timbuktu to join the salt caravans. Twice a year they set out on the 800-mile desert trail to Teghaza and Taoudenni, and brought back over 2,000 tons. This was pure rock salt, in the form of slabs weighing about 65 pounds each, white and smooth as marble.

From Timbuktu the salt was carried by canoe upstream to Jenne-jeno, from there

Indigo robe, handwoven belt, and distinctive knife are icons of Tuareg resourcefulness in the Sahara.

by donkey to the forest edge, and then by human porters through the forest to distant settlements. At each stage its value was inflated by the costs of transportation. By the time a slab of Saharan salt had reached Kong in what is now the Ivory Coast, or Gonja in modern Ghana, it had traveled nearly 1,200 miles and was as much an article of prestige as of utility. Arabs visiting Mali in the tenth century reported that to avoid waste, rock salt was always licked, never ground.

For every last grain of salt that came into the region, however, something of equivalent value had to go out. Ivory was one item that found a ready market, providing farmers with an income from the elephants that they were constantly chasing from their fields. Another was the kola nut, an addictive stimulant whose bitter taste relieved thirst and became a symbol of hospitality throughout the Sahelian and Saharan regions of West Africa. By the 13th century it was regularly carried across the Sahara to markets in North Africa—and thence even farther afield. By the 21st century the influence of the kola nut had embraced the planet as an ingredient of the world's most popular soft drink: Coca-Cola.

Today there are about 1.5 million Tuareg living in the Saharan regions of Algeria, Mali, and Nigeria. The northern Tuareg, custodians of the Tassili-n-Ajjer paintings and the epitome of the blue-veiled warlords of the Sahara, are now comparatively few in number, and their traditional way of life is all but abandoned. During colonial times their camel caravans were replaced by convoys of trucks, but by hiring themselves and their camels to local tour operators and working as guides and cooks, they earned enough money to carry on a semblance of their former proud glory.

For the Tuareg in the southern Sahara, the situation is only marginally better. Though trucks are replacing camels on the salt routes, most of the trade is still left to the Tuareg and their camels—but even they struggle to cover their costs. Recent caravans have been a financial struggle for Mahmouda, whose family gave up the seminomadic way of life a generation ago and settled at the Timia Oasis in Niger. They grow maize, vegetables, and fruit, and keep goats and cattle. They have a herd of camels and each year set out on the 270-mile desert crossing to Bilma, where they buy salt to sell in the markets of northern Nigeria, another 370 miles to the south.

The round-trip takes five months. Ten men and 100 camels must walk up to 30 miles a day, often trudging through the sands for 16 hours at a stretch in temperatures that can rise to 120°F in the shade. The journey is planned with military precision, but things can still go wrong. Mahmouda vividly remembers a year when several of his salt-laden camels died of exhaustion before the caravan reached the markets. They and their cargo had to be abandoned in the desert, wiping out all hope of a profit that year. The trade is hard, and likely to get harder. Even so, Mahmouda agrees that his son should begin to learn the practice and secrets of the Tuareg salt trade. Adam is ten years old. No wonder he looks nervous as he leads the head camel away from the mountains and out into the desert.

In the far-gone days when Adam's ancestors decorated the cave walls of Tassili-n-Ajjer, the rains that drenched the Sahara fell even more heavily on the highlands of central Africa, where the Nile begins its journey to the Mediterranean. The onset of the wet period enlarged the river's catchment area considerably. Rivers from the Ethiopian highlands joined the flow, eventually contributing more than four times as much water as the central African highlands. The seasonal floods became huge, but as the river scoured a wider course for itself they became more predictable. Farmers who had retreated into the Nile Valley when the Sahara turned dry settled permanently on a plain enriched with silts washed down from the volcanic highlands of the south.

By 5,000 years ago the river's annual floods had created over 6,900 square miles of cultivable land in Egypt. This narrow strip of fertile land winding through the desert was inhabited by about half a million people, who were concentrated most densely downstream from present-day Aswan, and around the delta where Cairo is situated. Here the cultures of the Sahara and the Near East combined to give rise to a unique and astonishing civilization.

And so the Egyptians reaped the benefits of the Nile. They worked the land with the plow, and invented the *shadoof* (a simple cantilevered water bucket) and the *saqqiyah* (an ox-driven waterwheel) to raise water from the river and irrigate their fields. Surplus production endowed them with time enough to discover the principles of astronomy and mathematics, invent a written language, build the pyramids, and create numerous pictures and statues depicting their society. They worked with copper and gold. They hoarded gemstones and made exquisite jewelry. Yet they never advanced beyond the age of bronze. The smelting of iron was delayed in the Nile Valley, despite its proximity to Anatolia, where the technology was first developed. The reason was probably twofold: There was insufficient timber to supply the charcoal required to smelt metal, and they did not really need iron. Bronze farming implements were perfectly adequate for working the soft alluvial soils of the floodplain.

The Egyptians discovered the limitations of bronze, however, when they were overwhelmed in the seventh century B.C. by Assyrian forces wielding iron weapons. Assyrians, Greeks, Romans, Turks, French, and British occupied their lands until Egypt became a monarchy in 1923, and an independent republic in 1953. History flows on, but for how long can Egypt continue soaking up the beneficence of the Nile? The country's absolute dependence on the river that gives it life has never been more stark than it is today.

A hundred and fifty years ago, Egypt had five million acres of farmland and five million citizens. Now it has 7 million acres of farmland and 69 million citizens. If the present trend continues, by 2025 there will be over 95 million Egyptians, and they will all want food, water, services, a job, and somewhere to live. The trouble is that three-quarters of Egypt is barren desert, and the country's expanding population has been housed on the land that is fertile. Egypt already has to import six million tons of grain a year, and the situation is likely to get worse.

Land and water are still the most pressing issues in Egypt, but the country abounds with the testimony of past success. The constraints of a harsh desert environment and the blessings of an unpredictable river inspired the innovations upon which the Nile civilizations were founded. With that ribbon of green, humanity defied the desert. The monuments of ancient Egypt at Giza,

As night falls in the desert between Fachi and Bilma, the temperature drops dramatically. Fires lit to cook the evening meal also provide welcome warmth for the men.

Memphis, and Luxor show what those ancient people were capable of doing, and their legacy persists.

So there is a measure of hope in the knowledge that many of the plants, animals, fish, and birds that the ancient Egyptians depicted in their paintings can still be found in the region. Farmers tend their rows of crops to the cooing of palm doves, the cries of the crested lark, and the call of the hoopoe—birds that were here 5,000 years ago. Ducks and painted snipe fly into the lagoons at dusk, herons stalk the shallows, and swallows skim the water, taking on fuel for the final stage of their flight from Africa to Europe— perhaps to nest under the gables of that village I knew in Wales.

At Timia, a Tuareg village in the foothills of the Air Mountains in Niger, Salahou is helping to load the camels. Tomorrow the caravan will set off for the Bilma Oasis, a journey of 270 miles across the sands and shifting dunes of the Sahara—some of the cruelest terrain on Earth. It will be months before Salahou sees home again.

t he Tuareg are the undisputed lords of the Sahara. No other people are so at home in the desert's featureless wastes. Swathed in robes of blue and indigo, guided by the stars, they have led camel caravans across the sands for centuries. Fiercely independent, their wanderings knew no boundaries, but only the camel made them possible.

The ships of the desert were introduced to the Sahara about 1,500 years ago. Surefooted, capable of going without water for days on end, camels enabled the Tuareg to become traders who ventured fearlessly into the Sahara's ocean of sand.

Tuareg caravans carried gold, ivory, and slaves across the Sahara from West Africa to the Mediterranean, returning with Arab and European luxury goods, and salt. The salt came from huge deposits left in the Sahara's ancient dried-out lakes and found ready markets in the forests and grasslands of West Africa, where natural supplies of salt are rare.

There was a time when the value of salt increased 60-fold over the 1,240-mile journey from mine to market. Salt from the desert bought gold from the forest. But the value fell as the volume of trade increased. By the 19th century, caravans up to 15 miles long were transporting 5,000 tons of salt a year from the desert. And in its turn, the 20th century brought yet more changes. Nowadays, many Tuareg are settled farmers. Some bring salt from the desert in trucks. But there are still a few who follow the traditional ways.

RAIN

forest

The tropical rain forest is a secretive place. Like a protecting veil, a vast green canopy conceals its mysteries from prying eyes, and an awesome tangle of trees, shrubs, vines, and creepers deters those who would trespass in its domain.

Though secretive and forbidding, the tropical rain forest throbs with the primeval essence of life on Earth. Through countless millennia, it has stood wherever warmth and moisture were sufficient, expanding and contracting with the changes of climate, but always preserving a precious store of life's diversity at its core. Unchanging in form while varying in size, the tropical rain forest stands as an icon of the stability and equilibrium of nature—an anchor for the spirit in a rapidly changing world.

Humans evolved from a forest-dwelling ancestor (and our closest cousins—the chimpanzees and gorillas—are there still), but evolutionary adaptations to the savanna environment left humanity poorly equipped for life in the forests. Fewer people live in the Congo Basin forests than in Kentucky, though they are 21 times larger than the state.

A new policy of selective felling may preserve the Cameroon rain forest. *FOLLOWING PAGES:* The designation Pygmy comes from the Greek work *pygme*, meaning "half an arm's length."

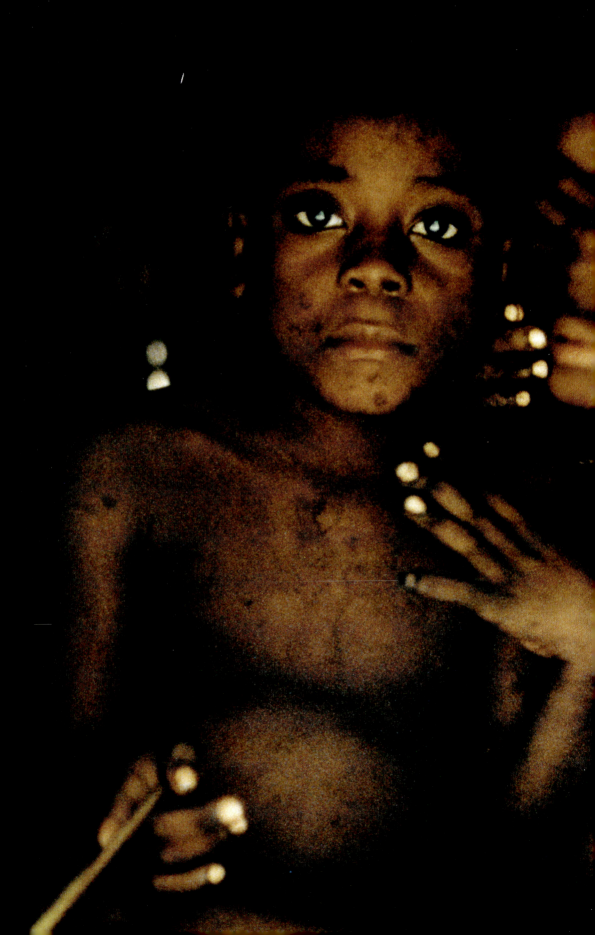

a t the height of the last major ice age, about 18,000 years ago, when one-third of the Earth's land surface was covered by glaciers up to three miles thick, the volume of water locked up in the ice caused sea levels to fall dramatically. The shores of Africa lay over 400 feet below present-day levels, and the southern tip of the continent was over 60 miles south of its present position.

With the Antarctic ice cap covering so much of the Southern Ocean, the temperature of the always chilly Benguela Current, which carries water northward along the Atlantic coast of Africa, plummeted. Evaporation from the colder water was reduced, and the southwest monsoon, which previously brought almost continuous rain to West Africa, was suppressed. The Sahara advanced 300 miles along its entire southern front during this dry period. Rivers ceased to flow, Lake Chad dried out, and even the Nile north of Khartoum was dammed by the advancing dunes. The sands of the Kalahari drifted all the way to the Congo River, 1,250 miles north of its present limits.

Not so long before, equatorial and tropical lowland rain forests had covered most of equatorial Africa. Now they were a string of isolated pockets in West and central Africa.

Africa has never again been as dry as during that last ice age. As the globe warmed up again, the forests reclaimed their former range, but the fragmentation of the African rain forest had a dramatic and lasting effect: It severely reduced the range of its plant life. Though packed with a challenging tangle of vegetation, there are fewer families, fewer genera, and fewer species of plants in Africa's rain forests than in either South America or Asia.

The human line has ancient links with the forest through the gorilla, although our distinctive adaptations evolved on the savanna.

My own first steps into an African rain forest were taken in the company of Nigerian troops during the Biafran War. Bullets were flying about, and I soon learned that the tactics upon which we depend for safety on the savanna or in a city are less helpful in the forest. You cannot see enough to feel safe. The rain forest is a generally dark and gloomy place. Even an occasional burst of sunlight tends to darken shadows more than it illuminates the ground it strikes. Trees and leaves are always obstructing the view. A Biafran soldier (or a leopard) could be lurking in the thicket, and I wouldn't have known until it was too late. And amid the trees there is no

sense of scale. Distances are difficult to judge. Move 30 feet in any direction and you could be completely lost. As I huddled with the platoon in a tangle of vines and thick-leaved shrubs, I could imagine that, for forest-dwelling animals, hearing, smell, and touch are far more useful than vision.

But although the tropical rain forest is a foreign place to most of us, there are few places on Earth that give such a compelling sense of life's exuberant fecundity. In the equatorial regions the amount of sunshine and the number of daylight hours varies only a little from day to day. Average temperatures are in the region of 77°F throughout the year. Some rain falls on most days, adding up to an annual average of between 60 and 100 inches overall. Such constant warmth and moisture has blanketed these regions with the largest volume of vegetation on Earth.

Trees are the rain forest's crowning glory. Soaring high enough to shade the windows of a 21st-floor apartment, each tree in the forest is the winner of endless battles with thousands of other organisms. Every mahogany tree that holds a place in the canopy is the sole survivor from tens of thousands of seeds. The intensity of that struggle is demonstrated by the number of different tree species that are found in the rain forest; virtually every tree in sight could belong to a different species. More than 200 different species have been counted in a 12-acre block.

But while our respect for these awesome trees might engender a belief that the rain forest has much to give, it is actually extremely selfish. Self-sustaining and generous to its own, it gives very little away. Nothing is wasted. The nutrient content of compost accumulating on the forest floor is rapidly channeled back into the living vegetation by dense networks of shallow feeder roots, a process so thorough that forest groundwater can be purer than commercial distilled water. And to cap it all, the rain forest even makes its own weather, since the massive banks of clouds that form from the water vapor rising from the trees seldom drift beyond the forest boundaries—most of the rain they release falls right back on the forest itself.

Furthermore, since the rain forest consists principally of standing trees, where nutrients are locked away for hundreds of years in a form that is totally inedible to all but the most specialized insects, only 2.5 percent of its biomass is directly available as food for herbivores. This simple fact explains why rain forest mammals, though many in terms of species, are few in individual numbers.

People are the least numerous of all— though the number of Pygmies who thronged to an elephant kill observed by Harvard zoologist Richard Wrangham in the Ituri Forest of the Congo Basin might have suggested the forest was bursting with people. This was a rare event. Word spread rapidly, and people from camps near and far soon gathered around the carcass. Excitement was intense as the animal was skinned and dismembered. Amid the din, patterns of negotiation became discernible. The hunters and those with immediate rights to a share were told to honor the obligations of kinship. Old debts and favors were settled in exchange for meat; new pledges were contracted. The talking went on for hours, doubtless reinforcing a web of reciprocal obligation that was fundamental to the social order of the region.

This incident eloquently demonstrates the value of cooperative behavior in human society, especially in the rain forest, where the scarcity of food has made it difficult for humans to establish a permanent presence. Though it's true that we evolved from a forest-dwelling ancestor, we subsequently moved out on to the savanna, where we became dependent on high-energy and protein-rich foods. The African rain forest is almost totally devoid of the foods that constitute the greater part of the human diet.

In fact, though there are more than 30 plants used as food in Africa, none was originally a forest plant. Even the yam, now a staple food throughout the rain forest regions of West Africa, was originally a savanna plant. So it was only with the introduction of food crops from other parts that people could live for any length of time in the forest, and even then, human occupation has always been limited. The rain forests of the Congo Basin, for example, support just over 3.1 million people—which seems a lot until one considers that over 700 million live in the same area of land in India.

Hunters were the first to establish a presence in the African rain forest, and their descendents are known today by a number of names according to the region they occupy, such as the Mbuti in the north Congo Basin and the Baka of the Cameroon forests. But to most of us they are known collectively as Pygmies.

The earliest known reference to a living Pygmy comes from the records of an expedition sent into the depths of Africa by King Neferkare over 4,000 years ago. A progress report described "a dancing dwarf of the god from the land of the spirits"; the king was intrigued and ordered that they should be looked after and brough back to Egypt immediately.

Earliest modern references are less complimentary, describing the Pygmies as "remnants of a declining race," who once had lived as independent hunters and gatherers but were now so degenerate that they depended upon villagers living nearby for their survival. But subsequent research convincingly indicates that no Pygmies have ever lived permanently and alone in the deep forest.

The ancestors of the Pygmies probably had lived around the fringes of the forest, where they enjoyed the best of two worlds: immediate access to foods from the savanna, and ample opportunity to hunt and gather in the forest. When herders brought their cattle onto the savanna and farmers settled on the more fertile areas, the Pygmies turned more and more to the forest for their subsistence. They developed links of mutual benefit with the farmers and herders, exchanging honey, meat, and labor for the essential foods the forest could not provide. Thus a bond was forged that enabled both hunter and farmer to move deeper into the forest than either could have done alone. They followed the rivers and elephant trails,

clearing stands of primary forest to establish villages and gardens. The Pygmies continued with their more nomadic ways, returning regularly to exchange the produce of the hunt (protein) for the produce of the garden (carbohydrates).

The farming villagers with whom the Pygmies traded were the vanguard of a little-known movement of peoples that is unmatched in human history: the Bantu migration. In the space of a few thousand years the Bantu transformed the human landscape of sub-Saharan Africa from a region thinly inhabited by scatterings of hunters and gatherers to one that was dominated by farmers living in villages. But this was not a conquest, nor even a migration, properly speaking. It was the dispersal of an expanding population. As one village was established and grew, some of its inhabitants moved on to establish another.

The cradle lands of the Bantu people were what is now the border region of Nigeria and Cameroon, where they cultivated the rich soils of the forest margins. Their dispersal began slowly about 5,000 years ago, advancing at an overall rate of no more than 15 miles each decade. Once beyond the forest, however, the rate of expansion accelerated. Bantu farmers were well established in the Great Lakes region of central Africa by 2,500 years ago and had reached the coast of southern Africa and the limit of their dispersal about 900 years later—in the fourth century A.D. In little

more than 3,000 years the Bantu had colonized virtually all of sub-Saharan Africa, from the savannas of the Sahel along the southern fringe of the Sahara to the southwest corner of the continent.

Biasa village lies on a road through the Ituri Forest that would hardly qualify as a cart track elsewhere. Baruwani was waiting and anxious to leave as soon as I clambered down from the truck. Although his group of Pygmy hunters regularly traded with the Biasa villagers, an air of mutual distrust prevailed. The Pygmies never stayed in village longer than necessary.

Baruwani's camp was an hour's walk into the forest. The women built a hut for me soon after we arrived, lacing large oval leaves onto the dome-shaped framework of fresh saplings so effectively that hardly a drop of rain came through during a storm that afternoon.

There were seven men and seven women in Baruwani's group, who between them had eleven children—nine less than five years old. In the evening seven fires would burn. While the children continued with their games or made bows to shoot arrows at

OPPOSITE: **Elephants are the architects of the rain forest. In their daily rounds of feeding, drinking, and socializing, they create trails and clearings that the rains may turn into streams and water holes.**

makeshift targets, the adults were constantly on the move—fetching wood and water, unwrapping their stock of cassava and leaves, and preparing forest mushrooms and scraps of meat for the pot. There was little if any discussion, no apparent schedule, but a well-ordered system gradually became apparent. Firewood, water, food—all arrived at each of the fire places and was prepared without fuss. When the food was ready, each family group gathered to eat at its fire. Darkness had fallen by the time the meal was finished.

Baruwani's group had occupied the camp for nearly two months when I visited, and it was looking distinctly lived-in. The huts were shedding their leaves, and the ground was littered with a mess of fireplaces, old leaves, pawpaw skins, and scatterings

Strips of bark or palm frond are intricately woven into a strong but lightweight basket.

of palm-nut husks—demonstrating a fundamental principle of the hunter-gatherers' nomadic lifestyle. Staying in one place for too long is unhealthy. Yes, Baruwani confirmed, the group would be moving soon.

Epidemic diseases are the scourge of humanity, and they are most prevalent where enough people are constantly in close contact. The small number and scattered distribution of our earliest ancestors limited the capacity of any infection to become rooted in the population, where it could attack generation after generation, but agriculture and the establishment of permanent villages swept aside this natural limitation. Crucially, the Bantu farmers who settled in the forests created the conditions that enabled malaria to get a hold on the human population. Previously, the mosquitoes that carry the disease had taken their blood meals from wild animals, but people became a new source of food as pioneer farmers converted stretches of forest into the kind of open, moist, and well-vegetated environment that the insects preferred. Before long a species evolved that preferred human blood: *Anopheles gambiae*. Unhappily, *Anopheles gambiae* carries the parasite that causes the most virulent form of malaria: *Plasmodium falciparum*.

Malaria originated in Africa, but today it is a worldwide public health problem. More than 40 percent of the global population lives in areas where they are at risk from the disease. It is particularly dangerous during pregnancy, causing severe anemia that often leads to the death of the mother and her unborn child. In regions where malaria is endemic, nearly all children are infected by the time they are two years old and thereafter can expect to suffer an average of six bouts a year. Many die, often less than three days after developing the first symptoms. Those who survive are drained of vital nutrients, impairing their physical and intellectual development. The disease hits families in rural areas especially hard, reducing their ability to work the land by more than half. Overall, the costs of malaria in Africa south of the Sahara are estimated at more than two billion dollars per year.

Meanwhile, though, the human organism itself has not been entirely passive in the face of malaria. As *falciparum* malaria attained unparalleled levels of intensity in the rain forests of West Africa, observers noticed that while practically all newcomers to infested regions became seriously ill soon after being bitten, large numbers of people who lived there all the time seemed to escape infection. Further investigation revealed that they possessed a physiological adaptation that gave them a measure of resistance against malaria—the sickle cell. People with this resistance inherit an abnormal form of hemoglobin that causes their blood cells to become crescent or sickle shaped. These cells rupture when the malaria parasite invades them, thus denying the parasite a place to multiply.

The advent of the sickle cell has been described as an example of human evolution in progress—a genetic response to an environmental threat. But the advantage did not come without a cost. The distorted sickle cells can also block capillaries and cause a variety of dangerous conditions, ranging from mild anemia to heart failure. The dangers are particularly high among individuals who inherit the sickle-cell gene from both parents. Most of these victims die in infancy from what is known as sickle-cell anemia. But those who inherit the gene from just one parent are endowed with a degree of resistance to malaria. And so, if all are not to die of sickle-cell anemia, each new generation must contain a high number of individuals who have survived malarial infection but do not have the gene. Indeed, the incidence of the sickle cell is generally not more than 20 percent of the population.

Despite the problems of malaria, Bantu farmers established numerous villages and small towns in the rain forest as they spread from their cradle land. In some instances a combination of history and environmental circumstance fostered the emergence of large states with an urban center and a single ruler—in a word, kingdoms. The city and state of Benin, for instance, originated nearly 3,000 years ago from the consolidation of farming settlements in the forests of what is now southeast Nigeria. At its height, Benin's rulers were powerful enough to

Now the Baka people of the Cameroon rain forest are settled permanently in Bosquet village. Their houses are roofed with corrugated iron, the walls a framework of thin poles plastered with red mud.

order the construction of a massive defensive ditch and wall around the city—seven miles in circumference and over 50 feet from the bottom of the ditch to the top of the surviving wall. The human effort involved in these earthworks was equal to that of an army of 1,000 men working 10 hours a day for 30 months. And the construction did not stop there. In the tangled vegetation surrounding the modern Benin City, there remains evidence of a vast network of enclosures, covering an area of about 2,500 square miles in total and linked one to the other by nearly 10,000 miles of earthworks. This is one of the greatest works of urban construction in the nonindustrial world. Far more material was moved than was used to build the Giza Pyramids, and, given a 40-hour week, the work would have kept 1,000 men busy for 150 years.

A Dutch traveler who visited Benin City around 1600 described its main street as "a great broad street, not paved, which seemeth to be seven or eight times broader than the Warmoes street in Amsterdam." Benin by that time was an established city-state with thousands of residents, supplied with food by farmers owing obeisance to the *oba*, whose status approached that of a divine king. He was never seen, except as

The tangle of vines, saplings, and buttresses of mature trees at ground level in the Bosquet community forest is a hint of the vitality that soars above.

a veiled figure in ceremonies acknowledging his power and authority. His rule was absolute—the life and death of every man, woman, and child was at his whim.

Craftsmen were employed to make artifacts reflecting the authority of the oba and the state. In particular, hundreds of bronze plaques (most now the prized treasure of museums around the world) adorned the walls of the oba's palace and administrative buildings, depicting scenes of ceremony, ritual, and conquest in a unique stylized manner. The exquisite detail and finish of these plaques demonstrate skills in crafting and casting that must have taken

generations to acquire. Such dedication to a specialized craft can only have been possible in a society that did not expect its craftsmen to be farmers as well—in other words, a stratified society. And here we touch on the dark side of Benin history: the slave trade.

The enslavement of subject peoples was an established feature of African society. Indeed, Benin could not have achieved so much without them. Nor could the Asante of present-day Ghana, who so willingly bought the thousands of slaves that Portuguese traders shipped across from Benin, as previously described. Benin and

Asante were the two most powerful kingdoms in West Africa when European traders arrived. Both engaged in trade with the newcomers, but the Asante had the most to offer, since their territory was one of the few parts of Africa where valuable minerals and abundant farming potential were found together.

Kumasi, the Asante capital situated on the fringe of the rain forest in northern Ghana, was the center of a trading empire that, at its maximum extent of more than 96,500 square miles in 1820, was larger than present-day Oregon. Goods were transported from Kumasi via a trade network that also facilitated Asante control of its subjugated territories. Although Asante was a militaristic society, the kingdom's strength lay in its political institutions. Asante integrated the king and local chiefs in a national council. The Asantehene was king in council, but he was chosen from among matrilineal candidates by the queen mother and prominent chiefs—a system that averted the dangers of succession disputes that have plagued other states in Africa and abroad.

Still, gold was the main reason for the long-term stability of the Asante state. The amount of gold mined is legendary. Even today Asante gold puts Ghana tenth in the league of world producers—only eighteen percent of South Africa's production but still enough to be the country's foremost foreign-exchange earner. In the early 19th century, European visitors noted that in one group of mines each miner was expected to produce two ounces daily; in another, 10,000 slaves were employed. Slanting pits were dug to depths approaching 165 feet. The ore was collected in calabashes or baskets and passed along a human chain to the surface, where it was crushed, washed, sieved, and packaged.

Everything, even a few bananas, had its price in gold. When converted into slave labor, gold enabled Asante to conquer the encircling forest. When converted into muskets, it defended the kingdom against its enemies. Provinces paid annual tributes of up to 18,000 ounces. A poll tax of one-tenth of an ounce was collected from every married man in each village. The courts imposed gold fines; the innocent were expected to make a thanks offering and the guilty could buy their acquittal. The Asantehene assured himself of the allegiance of ambitious followers by binding them to him with loans of gold. Heavy death duties prevented rich men from establishing personal dynasties. Wealth accumulated by an appointed chief belonged to his chiefdom or the state, not his descendants. In short, gold gave Asante a means of harnessing individual competitiveness into the service of the state.

Eyewitness accounts from the early days of European encounters with the Asante give an impression of so much activity that readers might be inclined to assume the

Celebrating the 25th anniversary of his ascension to the Golden Stool, the Asantehene,
Otumfuo Poku Ware II, is carried shoulder high in a pageant of color and gold.

region was very densely populated. But in fact, the region was always thinly populated, simply because farming in the rain forest is not very productive. Forest soils are not rich in nutrients. Farmers must continually clear new land, which they cultivate for 2 or 3 years, then leave fallow for up to 25 years while the natural vegetation grows back and rejuvenates the soils. Under the traditional system of shifting agriculture, as it is known, the forest was always a mosaic of cultivated land and clearings in various states of fallow. Because of this, it was thinly populated. Even the 6,500 square miles of the "metropolitan" Asante homeland around Kumasi supported only about 425,000 people.

FOLLOWING PAGES: **The Baka grow cassava in forest clearings. Introduced to Africa by the Portuguese, the plant's tuberous roots are rich in starch, but contain poisons that must be leached from the flour to make it edible.**

The point is that farming in the rain forest was extensive, not intensive. A relatively small number of people used a large area of land. Unfortunately, outsiders consistently assumed that the resources of forest not currently occupied were there for the taking, especially the trees, and especially during the 20th century, when vast areas of forest in West Africa were cleared. But it's not all bad news. The rain forest is one of the world's most dynamic ecosystems. It has a tremendous capacity to regenerate and is not easily suppressed, as the people farming it have known for generations. Indeed, there are places where it has actually advanced. Ancient termite mounds standing in the forests of eastern Ghana, for example, show that the region had been savanna grassland in the not so distant past, for mound-building termites live exclusively in the savanna. Likewise, archaeological evidence indicates that the city of Kumasi has not always been surrounded by dense rain forest.

The problems of rain forest loss are serious, but exaggeration helps no one. Accurate statistics and a fuller understanding of the forest's immense potential to regenerate could engender realistic hope and eliminate the prevailing air of despair.

Cameroon has taken a step in the right direction. Although a larger proportion of its forest has been logged than in any other African country, logging generally has been selective, taking only mature timber and rarely felling all the standing trees. Some areas have been logged three or four times, as trees progressively reached maturity.

The amount of timber felled increased dramatically during the late 1980s and 1990s, however, as Cameroon's economy took a downturn. Not all this logging was as careful as it should have been, but much of the forest remains capable of regenerating. That means closer control of access to the forests and of methods of cutting. And who better to do it than the people who live in the forest? The Baka's knowledge of their territory and its resources is encyclopedic. The rain forest is no Eden, but the Baka are supremely well adapted to life in its testing environment.

For centuries the Baka survived by sharing whatever the forest had to offer, among themselves and with Bantu farmers settled in the forest. They had learned that survival depended on the judicious husbanding of resources for communal benefit. In recent years, however, life for the Baka has been transformed. Government agencies and Christian missionaries persuaded them to settle in villages permanently. They adopted the lifestyle of the Bantu farmers and abruptly moved from a way of life based on mutual support and sharing to one based on personal profit. At first they were easily exploited because they did not understand the rules of the game. The forests were logged without consultation, and the Baka received none of the revenue.

Dirt roads through the heart of the Cameroon rain forest were made primarily for the logging industry. Regions have been heavily logged, but the forest will regenerate where only mature trees are felled.

But they quickly adapted to the new circumstances. The Baka who had settled in Bosquet village, for example, successfully petitioned for the surrounding rain forest to become a protected community forest, managed by themselves. They—better than anyone else—understood that management was the best option, not a blanket ban on logging. After all, people have been using the African rain forest for centuries. In the past, a tree was felled only to make room for crops and houses. Nowadays, the incentive is timber, and demand is high. But the forests can be logged in a sustainable manner to the benefit of everyone—from the forest dweller to the city dweller whose dining table gleams with the richness of the rain forest.

t

o the Baka people, the mysterious depths of the Congo rain forest are home. The ancient Egyptians knew of these forest dwellers and called them "people of the trees." Early explorers called them "Pygmies" on account of their small stature. The Baka say they have lived here longer than anyone knows. They even have a legend that tells how their ancestors were thrown out of heaven for being too noisy and sent to liven up the forest. Ever since, their voices, laughter, and music have brought the warmth of humanity to the forbidding forest.

The rain forests of the Congo Basin are built on a scale that humbles the human spirit. So big, yet offering so little opportunity for people. Warmth and ample rainfall keep this equatorial heart of Africa thumping with deep, enduring power, but nearly all the forest's bounty is locked up in huge trees that only insects can eat. And the trees use available resources so efficiently that the ground on which they stand is virtually devoid of nutrients. Little is left to sustain other living things. Only ingenuity and a long history of custom and tradition have enabled the Baka to thrive in the forest, generation after generation.

But now the Baka's traditional way of life is threatened. The huge forest trees that stood for centuries as the unchanging reality of their very existence are being felled for the global market in exotic hardwoods. The demand is high, but the Baka have turned it to their advantage. Having successfully petitioned the government for community control of their forest, they now plan to manage it for sustainability as well as profit.

Humanity has been its most resourceful in the rain forest. Fired from his crossbow, the slim dart Richard Kadjama holds in his mouth will slip swiftly and silently through the undergrowth to spear the unsuspecting target—a bird or small mammal.

m

OUNtaINS

Africa's high mountains stand like far-flung islands in a sea of savanna and lowland forest—grand relics of the Earth's ancient turmoil, where altitude and isolation conspire to create taxing environments for all forms of life. Equatorial sun and thin air bring scorching summer every day and freezing winter every night to the heights of Africa's highest mountains. On Kilimanjaro, a climb from the savanna foothills to the summit glaciers is akin to traveling from the Equator to the Pole in the space of a few miles.

Forests of heather and alpine moorlands studded with giant groundsels and lobelias are some of the plant kingdom's wondrous adaptations to these extreme environments, while the bleeding heart baboon and the Ethiopian wolf are two animals uniquely adapted to life on the heights. Among people, social and cultural adaptations are often a response to environmental constraints, and a remarkable history of human fortitude and resilience has sprung from the isolated mountain fortresses of Ethiopia.

The Blue Nile carves a winding canyon through the high mountain landscape of Ethiopia. *FOLLOWING PAGES:* A clay hair bun crowned with an ostrich feather denotes a man's high reputation and courage for the Karo farmers of southwest Ethiopia.

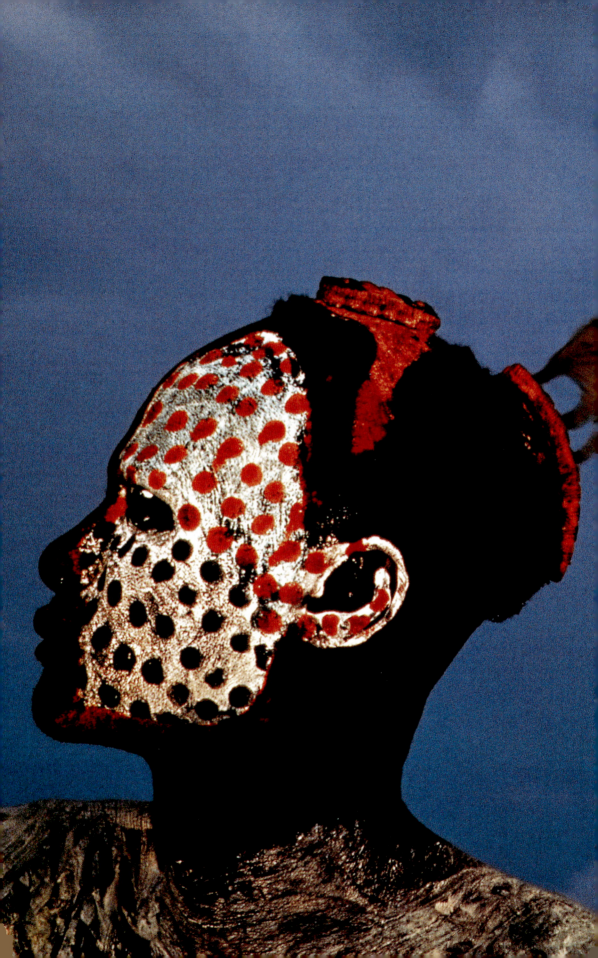

D

awn, and as the sun breaks through the piercing chill of night on the plain outside Korem, Ethiopia, it lights up a biblical famine, now, in the 20th century. This place, say workers here, is the closest thing to hell on Earth. Thousands of wasted people are coming here for help. Many find only death. They flood in every day from villages hundreds of miles away, felled by hunger, driven to the point of desperation. Death is all around.

The BBC television news report of October 23, 1984, was broadcast around the world.

Famine had struck in Ethiopia—again. Pictures of cruelly emaciated children, of mothers brushing the flies from the eyes of dying babies, of fathers digging graves, evoked memories of previous Ethiopian famines. Thousands of people—most of them farmers and families with a proud history of self-sufficiency—were reduced to the indignity of holding out begging bowls. The world responded generously, contributing millions of dollars to famine relief. But what was going on? Was the famine simply a consequence of drought, or were farmers abusing the land in their attempt to feed an expanding population? Was the drought a first sign of global warming? Or was something more sinister afoot?

In recent times, drought and famine, political upheaval, and civil war have made Ethiopia an icon of human distress, but in the distant past, its location and unique ecological circumstance fostered the evolution of especially resilient characteristics. Among its people, the trials of life on the high plateaus created traditions of robust faith that became the rallying points for opposition against despotic rulers.

The famine that Ethiopia had suffered in 1973 is a case in point. Up to 200,000 people died. The government of Emperor Haile

Ethiopia's present population of nearly 66 million is expected to double in the next 25 years. The future of the country rests with its children.

Selassie refused to acknowledge the problem, as indeed it had ignored famines in 1958 and 1966. But this time the famine was more serious, and the situation became critical when city dwellers, students, and junior army officers seized upon the famine as a symbol of the need for political change. The government was overthrown. Emperor Haile Selassie was assassinated. Government ministers and administrators were imprisoned. Col. Mengistu Haile Mariam became the head of government, and soon thereafter, new legislation stripped wealthy landowners of their traditional rights. Their lands were distributed among the peasants, who until then had farmed for their masters in conditions of feudal penury, never far from starvation.

Mengistu was said to have "emerged out of the belly of the Ethiopian masses" and was heartily welcomed at first. He eventually fell from favor as he murdered rivals and assumed powers in excess even of those whom the revolution had displaced, but his initial rise to power was an inspiring moment for Ethiopia.

In the afterglow of the revolution, the directors of the National Museum were persuaded that the museum should emphasize themes of national identity and unity. They commissioned a painting of a symbolic moment from the nation's history, and soon

Lalibela landscape, site of many rock-hewn churches, lies over 6,500 feet above sea level. Rugged and afflicted by drought, the region is noted for the deep religious conviction of its people.

the museum was adorned with a painting that showed the felling of a massive ancient tree, said to symbolize "the people's triumph over feudalism and backwardness."

But massive trees are now rare in Ethiopia. The forests of stately cedar and juniper that once covered almost nine-tenths of the Ethiopian Highlands have gone, felled by an expanding population and its intensified exploitation of the environment. Although the highlands constitute less than half of Ethiopia's land area, they are home to nearly 90 percent of the country's population. Furthermore, almost all of Ethiopia's cropland is situated in the highlands, along with two-thirds of its livestock.

Some ancient junipers survive, if only because they stand behind the protective walls of a church compound, where cutting a tree is akin to desecration. Still, these trees are a sorry sight. Standing alone, with their spindly branches reaching out like wasted limbs, they look like elderly citizens silently lamenting their fate.

Ethiopia is the most mountainous corner of Africa. Almost 80 percent of Africa's land above 9,800 feet is here, though the country comprises barely 4 percent of the continent's total land surface. The Ethiopian mountains were formed by the huge upheavals and volcanic activity that also created the East Africa Rift Valley. For millions of years, volcanoes spewed sheets of lava over the landscape; then, as the volcanoes quieted down five million years ago, the barren mountains were increasingly subjected to the depredations of climate. Glaciers scoured the heights. The sun baked the lava fields of the plateau. Wind and rain sculpted a mesmeric landscape of peaks and canyons, precipices, and jagged fans of ridges and gullies. As with the Grand Canyon, the Ethiopian mountain landscape evokes a humbling sense of awe.

The Ethiopian massif is relatively young, geologically speaking, and this, combined with its isolation and unique environments, created an ecological vacuum. Colonists from other parts of the continent rapidly evolved here into species that are found nowhere else. Thus Ethiopia is home to a number of endemic animals and plants, including the highland rose (*Rosa abyssinica*), which has sweet-smelling leaves as well as flowers; the African primrose (*Primula verticillata*); the blue-winged sheldgoose (*Cyanochen cyanoptera*), whose ancestors arrived long ago from the alpine grasslands of South America; and the Malcolm's earless toad (*Nectophryonoides malcolmi*), which is found only at altitudes of between 10,500 feet and 13,000 feet.

Among mammals, the mountain nyala and the Walia ibex also thrive in the Ethiopian Highlands. And the cliffs of the northern massif are where Ethiopia's most colorful animals are found on wet, chilly evenings, huddled together in their thick waterproof coats—gelada baboons. Also known as the "bleeding heart" monkey for the distinctive patch of bare, pink skin on its breast, the gelada is a grass-eating mammal that must devote most of its waking hours to eating if it is to get all the sustenance it needs from its low-quality diet. Fortunately, there is plenty of grass, and few other animals competing for it; only the time in which to eat is limited.

Because they must spend so much time eating, gelada troops are remarkably orderly; there is little of the squabbling seen among other monkeys. Significantly, they eat sitting down, which saves energy and conserves warmth but also hides a socially important part of primate anatomy: the rear end. Among apes in particular, genital gesturing (presenting, as ethologists put it) is part of the everyday social order, used to appease aggression and offer friendly greetings.

A necklace of cowrie shells graces the clothing of a farmer's wife in the Ethiopian Highlands. Cowrie shells, dredged from the lagoons of the Maldive Islands, were once the currency of the slave trade.

And of course, it enables males to watch out for the reddened vulva that indicates a female coming into estrus.

By sitting all day to eat and save energy, the geladas have lost this means of monitoring the sexual readiness of females. But in a remarkable instance of evolutionary ingenuity, the gelada females have developed an area of bare skin around the breasts and up to the neck that reddens and swells at the same time that the vulva reddens and swells; the process is triggered by the same hormones and indicates umistakably that the female is primed to reproduce. Males also develop the bare pink breast, but for

them it serves only to attract or repel individuals of both sexes.

The highlands were not inhabited by significant numbers of people until about 7,000 years ago, when changes in climate brought prolonged drought to the plains. Moving onto the heights, farmers and herders found an environment that was highly conducive to human settlement. The temperature range is congenial, and the diseases common in the lowlands, such as malaria, trypanosomiasis, and bilharzia,

Injera, made from teff, is prepared for a wedding feast. Teff contains more essential minerals than other grains; its nutritional value is enhanced by preparation, which generates additional vitamins.

are absent. The tsetse fly, which makes cattle raising impossible in much of Africa, is not found in the cool highlands. Furthermore, moisture-laden winds from the Red Sea produce nourishing rains.

As with the environment, the vegetation seems expressly intended for human exploitation. The Ethiopian Highlands contain more indigenous plants that can be used for food than any other part of Africa. There is the endemic false banana, *ensete (Musa ventricosa)*; the oil-producing *nug (Guizotia abyssinica)*; the Oromo potato *(Plectranthus edulis)*; the seeds of the safflower *(Carthamus tinctorius)*; and *sensel*

(Adhatoda schimperiana), whose pungent-smelling leaves are used to treat malaria. And then, of course, there is coffee *(Coffea arabica)*, a bush whose berries have been the main ingredient of a refreshing beverage for 2,000 years.

But while coffee stimulated the mind, it was the cereals that did most to feed the body. Finger millet *(Eleusine coracana)* probably originated in Ethiopia, and distinct types of wheat, barley, and sorghum were introduced from elsewhere—probably from the Nile or across the Red Sea—and grown locally. The cereal that contributed most to the historical development of the region, however, was of purely Ethiopian origin: teff (*Eragrostis tef*). First cultivated on the plateau, it fueled a civilization whose size and sophistication were unmatched in sub-Saharan Africa. Even today, teff is sown on more land than any other crop in Ethiopia.

The fields of teff that dominate the northern Ethiopian landscape in the aftermath of the rainy season look more like hay meadows than a cereal crop just a few weeks from harvest. The plant is light and delicate, and the grain it produces is tiny. But the carbohydrate and protein content of teff matches that of maize, sorghum, wheat, and barley. Even more importantly, it is particularly rich in the amino acids that the body cannot make on its own.

During the 19th and 20th centuries, when recurring drought and famine devastated Ethiopia, the particular value of teff has been not so much its nutritional content as its capacity to produce a harvest when other cereals have failed. Because teff is uniquely adapted to the region's climate, it will develop and ripen grain from every pollinated flower even if no further rain falls while the plant is maturing. Non-indigenous cereals grown in Ethiopia ripen little or no grain under these conditions.

The bare pink breast of the gelada baboon is an adaptation to the demands of the species' mountainous habitat.

A sound agricultural base appears to have been established on the northern Ethiopian plateau by 500 B.C., and the buildings, tombs, altars, elaborate stone carvings, metalwork, and evidence of writing revealed at archaeological sites all indicate that a complex society, most likely a state, was established there by the third century B.C. A town called Aksum was at the center. Nestling beneath a semicircle of low wooded hills, Aksum was beautifully situated, both in strategic and natural terms. A river flowed in from the north through a narrow cleft that was dammed to store water for the dry season. There was open ground for crops and grazing in the immediate vicinity, and the woods on the hills above provided timber for building and fuel. The dwellings of the wealthy occupied the higher elevations, and the artisans and lower classes lived below. Stone, quarried from the nearby hillside, was the material of choice for wealthy residents. Everyone else used mud-and-wattle construction, with roofs thatched with straw.

By the first century A.D. Aksum was the commercial and administrative center of an empire whose influence extended across the Red Sea to southern Arabia. Its rulers maintained close ties with the eastern Roman Empire and achieved prominence in the third century by issuing their own coinage in gold, silver, and bronze. Persian leaders of the day described Aksum as one of the world's four most important kingdoms; the other three were Persia, Rome, and Sileos (possibly meaning China).

Though situated high up on the plateau, about a hundred miles from the nearest access to the Red Sea, Aksum exported goods as far as India, China, the Black Sea, and Spain. Pliny the Elder, writing in the first century A.D., specifies ivory, rhinoceros horns, hippopotamus hides, and slaves as goods from Aksum. Other sources refer to gold dust, frankincense, civet cat musk, and even live elephants. By A.D. 500 the city of Aksum was more extensive and more densely populated than even its modern counterpart. Meanwhile, its rulers had developed what has been aptly described as a "mania for the gigantic."

From the beginning, Aksum had buried its rulers in stone-walled tombs and marked their graves with monumental stelae (or obelisks). Over 120 stelae have been located in the city, and all but a few have fallen. Most of the stelae are irregular in shape but perfectly smooth, with rounded edges and curved sides and shallow undulations along their length. Like works of sculpture, these stelae might have been carved to enhance the form of the natural stone.

But the six largest are very different, more indicative of an intention to revise rather than respect the stone's natural form. Each is precisely rectangular in section and elaborately decorated with bas-relief representations of multistoried buildings.

One of the larger examples still stands in a neatly tended park in present-day Axum (the town's modern spelling). It is a single block of granite 68 feet high, carved with geometric precision to represent a ten-story building. The fallen pieces of an even larger, similarly decorated stela were taken to Rome in 1937 during the Italian occupation of Ethiopia and reerected near the site of the Circus Maximus. (They have recently been returned to Ethiopia.) The largest of all—108 feet long and carved on all 4 sides to represent a 13-story building—lies broken in 5 huge pieces, with smaller fragments scattered about.

Whether this massive decorated piece of stone ever stood upright is uncertain. It weighed over 700 tons and was probably the largest single block of stone ever quarried, carved, and set up in the ancient world; transporting and then raising such a massive stone was an undertaking that would strain the ingenuity and technical resources even of modern engineers. Moreover, dressing the stone with the unsophisticated metal or stone tools of the time and cutting bas-relief designs between 4 and 8 inches deep into its entire surface area (roughly 3,550 square feet)

would have kept a sizable corps of masons busy for years.

No two of Aksum's six great stelae are identical, but when arranged in order of increasing size, each one is more elaborately decorated than the one before. This "mania for the gigantic" appears to have ended with the greatest of the six stelae, possibly because its fall was interpreted as a bad omen, possibly because its manufacture demonstrated the sheer impossibility of hewing, transporting, and raising anything larger. In any event, by the fourth century A.D. Aksum was moving in a direction that made further pursuit of the gigantic impossible. The city-state was destined to become a victim of its own success.

Over the centuries, the woodlands had been stripped bare. While clearing the forest for crops initially helped to feed a growing population, it also exposed the soils to overcropping and erosion. Ironically, the good rains that had nourished the growth of Aksum now hastened its decay. Nutrients were leached from the land as soil was washed from the hillsides.

There were also commercial and political difficulties abroad. War in the eastern Mediterranean reduced the market for luxury goods in the Roman Empire. Then Persia gained control of southern Arabia, threatening trade routes to India, and by the early eighth century Arab forces had cut Aksum's access to the Red Sea trade. Gold coinage ceased to be issued. Centralized power collapsed. Within a few generations Aksum and its satellite communities were reduced to loose clusters of villages. By A.D. 800 Aksum almost ceased to exist. People abandoned the impoverished landscape in favor of settlement on the virgin soils to the south, where they spurned the luxury grains brought in from southern Arabia and relied once again on teff. This move laid the foundations for the emergence of the modern Ethiopian state. In it, Aksum would become a symbol of ancient royal and religious authority—just as it is today.

"Biblical" was the word that immediately sprang to mind when I visited Axum. The roads are unmade, there are more carts and donkeys than motor traffic, and the people, dressed in homespun cloaks, wear sandals on their feet and carry a staff as they trudge through the sand. The sounds of human activity predominate, a striking contrast to the cacophony of mechanical noise that most urban dwellers tolerate. Away from the main thoroughfare, narrow paths wind between houses, where women are grinding teff and preparing *injera* over charcoal stoves. Their husbands work the fields, and their children tend the goats.

OPPOSITE: **Behind the door at Lake Tana's Narga Selassie Church, decorated with guardian angels, lies the Tabot, the replica Ark of the Covenant. The original ark was the chest containing the tablets on which God had written the Ten Commandments. Legend says that it was brought to Ethiopia by an early ruler and is kept in the Church of St. Mary, Axum.**

Aksum converted to Christianity only in the fourth century A.D., but Ethiopians claim that their connection with biblical events dates back to the ninth century B.C., when the Queen of Sheba is said to have traveled from her Ethiopian palace to meet King Solomon in Jerusalem; their meeting is described in the tenth chapter of the Book of I Kings. Ethiopian tradition interprets the scripture to mean that Solomon spent the night with the queen, and that she gave birth to Solomon's son upon her return to Ethiopia. The child was named David, and in due course he ascended to the throne as Menelik I, founder of the Solomonic dynasty. In later times, the link between Ethiopia and Christian religion was strengthened by a legend telling that, while still a young man, Menelik had brought the fabled Ark of the Covenant to Aksum.

The Ark of the Covenant was the most sacred object of Old Testament times, a strongbox made for the stone tablets on which the Ten Commandments had been written by the finger of God. This most potent artifact accompanied the Israelites through the wilderness, helping them to victory in every encounter. Legend says that, as a young man, Menelik spent a year at his father's court in Jerusalem, where the Ark resided, and that, on his departure, he stole the Ark and carried it back to Aksum, where it has remained ever since.

There is no other account of what happened to the Ark. Even the Bible is silent on the subject. But claims of its presence in Aksum are contradicted by historical fact, and the legend of Solomon, Sheba, and Menelik has no historical basis. The Queen of Sheba is a mythical figure. Aksum did not exist as a political entity while Solomon was alive, and the city itself was founded several centuries after Menelik supposedly brought the Ark to Aksum.

But belief is a powerful force. With the collapse of the Aksumite state, the church became the root of influence and authority in Ethiopia. Kings acquired divine status— the priest-king—and before long fabulous tales of Ethiopia and its monarchs reached Europe. Twelfth-century manuscripts refer to a powerful Christian priest-king named Prester John whose vast empire contained such wonders as the fountain of youth, a river whose bed consisted entirely of gemstones, ants that dug gold, pebbles that gave light or could make a man invisible, and a mirror that enabled Prester John to see anywhere in any one of his many kingdoms.

Likewise, Ethiopians took an interest in Europe and were exploring its city streets 100 years before the first European visited Ethiopia in 1407. The evidence is scanty, but a document found in medieval archives describes how a group of 30 Ethiopians on visits to Avignon and Rome in 1306 had been forced to wait at Genoa for a favorable wind to take them home. It is also known that Ethiopians regularly visited Egypt and Cyprus and made pilgrimages to the holy sites of Palestine, where they established links with the rest of the Christian world. These contacts gave Europeans exaggerated notions of the role the Ethiopians could play in an alliance against the Arab forces, which seemed determined to conquer all Europe.

King Henry IV of England sent a letter to the "king of Abyssinia, Prester John" in 1400, evidently seeking his participation in a crusade against Islam. It is not known if Henry's letter reached Ethiopia, but in 1402 King David sent envoys to Italy asking for technical aid and received a number of Florentine craftsmen at his court. Vatican records show that letters of safe conduct were given to at least three parties of Italians who traveled to Ethiopia between 1451 and 1453, and a traveler who visited Ethiopia in 1482 reported on his return that he had met 10 Italians there who had been in the country for 25 years. It is known that the French sent missions to Ethiopia as well.

These fragments of evidence add up to a clear indication that continuous relations were established between Ethiopia and Europe during the first half of the 15th century. Furthermore, the extent of Europe's knowledge of the land of Prester John is shown on two contemporary maps: the "Egyptus Novelo," probably drawn in Florence circa 1454, and the "Mappa Mundi," drawn in Venice in 1460. Both contain details of Ethiopian geography that must have come from firsthand sources. Even more significantly, the "Mappa Mundi"

shows Africa surrounded by ocean, ostensibly confirming the assumption that sailing around the continent was a practical idea.

Many of the stories about Prester John were myth, but the kings of Ethiopia were real enough. Their brand of Christian nationalism united the people of the Ethiopian Highlands, setting down roots from which a nation of remarkable durability has grown. Some of them were cruel despots who ruthlessly exploited the peasants, and though civil wars ravaged the country, none of this could destroy the state. Rulers and ruled alike believed in the ultimate sanction of the authority that was vested in the church. The words of God, written in stone and preserved in the Ark of the Covenant, lay in the dark recesses of the sanctuary at Aksum, and no Ethiopian was ever beyond their authority.

A replica of the ark is enshrined in each of Ethiopia's more than 20,000 Christian churches. Known as Tabots, these replicas play a central role in major religious events—particularly at the feast of Timkat, when the Tabot is carried in procession and the faithful bow and pray as it passes. A replica of the ark is used in the Timkat procession even at Axum, and thousands of

FOLLOWING PAGES: **At a wedding in Addis Ababa, young congregation members wear homespun cotton shifts and crowns of satin.**

people flock there for the festival. Crowds surge past the stelae, but make no gestures of respect—much less reverence—for those relics of their ancestral civilization. The evidence of the past is diminished by the promise that faith offers for the future.

The power of faith was something that the Communist-inspired Mengistu regime ignored when it took control from Haile Selassie in 1974. Though some of the reforms were welcomed, attempting to reduce the influence of the church was a step too far. As the totalitarian nature of the new regime began to show, religion provided a network of shared belief through which opposition could spread and consolidate.

Like history repeating itself, it was once again a famine that set the grounds for the Mengistu regime's collapse. The BBC television news report of October 23, 1984, focused world attention on the Ethiopian crisis, but unlike Haile Selassie's government during the famine of 1973, the Mengistu regime welcomed the international attention. The foreign media were only too ready to attribute the famine to drought and global warming, and so the regime was able to direct attention away from the government-directed population resettlement, economic upheaval, and civil war. Moreover, the large amounts of food aid flooding into the country provided a ready source of supplies for the Ethiopian army, which was fighting the secessionist Eritrean and Tigrean forces. In December 1984, acting Foreign Minister Tibebu Bekele told the U.S. chargé d'affaires, probably with more candor than he intended, that "food is a major element in our strategy against the secessionists."

Hundreds of thousands of Ethiopians died in the famine, and millions more were left destitute. The world responded to the catastrophe with unprecedented generosity, and the scale of the response seemed to herald a new era of global concern. That makes all the more tragic the heartless chicanery of the Mengistu government, which worked to ensure that the humanitarian effort prolonged the suffering more than alleviated it.

The relief program helped to keep Mengistu in power, but other factors were working against him. The crumbling of Communism in the late 1980s sharply reduced the military assistance Ethiopia had been receiving from the Soviet Union. In cities and towns across the country, opposition to his rule was mounting, with the church as the rallying point of protest. At Timkat during the final years of Mengistu's rule, the crowds straining for a glimpse of the Tabot were huge and determined—their devotion an expression of religious nationalism that could not be suppressed.

Mengistu slipped into Zimbabwe one day in May 1991, where he was received as a political refugee. Ethiopians took a breath, like weary travelers relieved of heavy burdens, then began tackling the country's problems with characteristic vigor. Korem,

St. George's Church is one of 11 hewn from the living rock—a relatively soft volcanic tuff—at Lalibela in the Ethiopian Highlands. Lalibela was chosen by a 12th-century ruler to be laid out as a new City of Zion.

known around the world as a symbol of disaster, soon became its former self—a small, peaceful trading village that served a far-flung community of farmers.

Returning home was not easy for the thousands who had crowded the refugee camps. They trudged back to their farms, weakened in body and spirit, with painful memories of the children and relatives they had left behind in graveyards. But even the climate was generous in the aftermath of the famine, bringing a sequence of exceptionally good rains. Farmers turned the soil, sowed the seed, and reaped the harvest. Before long they were on the road to Korem again—but this time not as refugees. Now they were successful farmers, with bags of grain for sale.

t

he high, craggy mountains of Ethiopia are the last refuge of the rare Walia ibex, gelada baboon, and endangered Ethiopian wolf. They also have been a haven for the world's major religions. Judaism, Islam, and Christianity have all found a home here. Their legacy has left a land replete with holy places.

Ethiopia embraced Christianity less than 400 years after the birth of Christ—while Europe was still in the Dark Ages. The church became the font of influence and authority throughout the country. Kings were accorded divine status—and became so famous that tales of the priest-king Prester John reached distant Europe. The Ark of the Covenant, the chest containing the tablets on which God wrote the Ten Commandments and therefore Christianity's holy of holies, is said to be in Ethiopia, taken from Solomon's Temple by a legendary Ethiopian king. A replica of the ark, called the Tabot, is kept in each of the country's 20,000-plus churches.

In the 12th century, a replica City of Zion was built at Lalibela. A hill in the city was named Calvary, and a stream flowing through it was called the Yordanos. Over the centuries, the devout have carved 11 churches from the solid rock at Lalibela. Each year, thousands flock to the town for the celebration of Timkat, the feast of Epiphany, when the Tabot is ceremoniously paraded from the churches to the baptism pool. For most who take part, a spray of holy water is the joyous culmination of Timkat. But for some young men, a place in the formal procession is a first step on the road to becoming a priest.

Ethiopia is a deeply spiritual country, where the authority of the church is widely respected by the country's 24 million Orthodox Christians.

saHeL

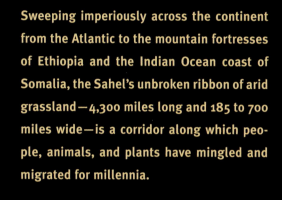

Sweeping imperiously across the continent from the Atlantic to the mountain fortresses of Ethiopia and the Indian Ocean coast of Somalia, the Sahel's unbroken ribbon of arid grassland—4,300 miles long and 185 to 700 miles wide—is a corridor along which people, animals, and plants have mingled and migrated for millennia.

Sahel is the Arabic word for "shore," and this is the shore of the Sahara Desert. Like a high-water mark that advances and recedes with the tide, the Sahel has moved south as climate change caused the desert to expand, and north again as the desert contracted. But throughout, the Sahel has endowed Africa with a ribbon of life-giving opportunity.

Cattle herders are the masters of the Sahel—the Fulani of Senegal and Mali, the Peuhl of Niger, the Dinka of Sudan, and the Samburu of Kenya. These are the nomadic pastoralists whose cattle graze on distant Sahelian ranges, converting a scanty crop of grass to a harvest of meat, milk, and calves that will enrich their home villages.

Harmattan winds fill the Dogon region of Mali with the promise of rain. *FOLLOWING PAGES:* Three young women head for the Daral festival in Diafarabé, Mali.

the cluster of huts was situated on the southern edge of the El Barta Plain, 6,500 feet above sea level. The air was cold in the early morning. In preparation for milking, Nankarusi warmed her hands in a stream of urine flowing from one of the cows, then laid the crudely stuffed skin of a calf killed by cheetahs the previous day before its mother, who nuzzled the surrogate form and obligingly let down her milk.

Nankarusi massaged the teats, then directed the milk into the long polished gourd. When the milking was finished and the herd had left the enclosure, she and the other women took handfuls of fresh dung that the cows had dropped overnight and plastered it over the walls of the huts, filling cracks, patching holes.

As the day advanced, a band of quivering heat rose from the ground. There was no sign of rain. Red sand, humps of gray scrub bush, acacia trees with thorns standing out from the bare branches like bleached fish bones—amid all the dryness the grazing cattle somehow found something to eat. But they had to drink too.

Lesipin, a man whose ability to interpret the stars was widely respected, had said that if rain did not fall before the horn of the Pleiades dropped below the horizon, there would be no rain at all that season. For the past week the clouds had been gathering— but then had thinned again, and the horn of the Pleiades had disappeared below the horizon the night before. The prospect of rain on the El Barta Plain was slim now, and the next chance of rain was four or five months hence.

Several herds were already drinking at the much depleted dam pond below Koitokol when Linolosi arrived there with his cattle, and not all of them were

The Niger River—artery of the western Sahel—has been traveled for centuries by traders between the cities and villages.

Samburu. Koitokol marks a point at which the Samburu territory merges with that of their neighbors, the Rendille and the Turkana, in northern Kenya. From the wall of the dam, other herds could be seen approaching across the plains: Turkana from the west, Rendille from the north and east, Samburu from the south and east.

When the rainfall is adequate, these three groups are kept apart by the different rangelands used by the different livestock they keep. The Samburu are able to keep cattle as well as sheep and goats in the highlands they occupy due to the relatively high rainfall. In the drier lowlands to the north of the Samburu territory, the Rendille can maintain only camels. The Turkana, who range around the southern end of Lake Turkana and into the furnace of the Suguta Valley, lead a much more opportunistic life, subsisting largely on sheep and goats but keeping cattle when they can.

It is ecology that keeps the three groups apart. Each subsists on the most productive stock that its territory can support. Yet for the people themselves the distinctions are first and foremost cultural.

The Rendille, or "people of the camel," share many affinities with the Samburu, "people of the cattle." The two groups are traditional allies against the Turkana, who are noted primarily for their lack of social cohesion. They do not circumcise, and they have few food taboos. They will even eat fish, say Samburu elders.

Now, at the height of a drought, the Turkana and the Rendille were invading Samburu territory. Grazing for Samburu cattle was running short, but there was still enough for camels and goats, which browse on bushes more than they graze. From the Rendille and Turkana point of view there was no choice. They had to move onto Samburu lands or watch their stock die. Their intrusion was not welcomed, though. At the dam, stories were told of the past, when bloody skirmishes broke out between Turkana and Samburu warriors.

As feelings ran dangerously high, the Samburu relieved the tension by driving their cattle up the tortuous tracks to

The fine work of Mali's expert goldsmiths is beautifully displayed at the Daral festival in Diafarabé.

the summit plateaus of Mount Nyiru, 9,000 feet above the plains. Here in grassy forest glades, the cattle flourished. Meanwhile, Rendille camels quickly moved in to browse on the scrubby vegetation that the Samburu had left behind, and the Turkana herded their livestock onto the territory vacated by the Rendille.

Though the pasture on Mount Nyiru is lush, even in the dry season,the Samburu

do not keep cattle there year-round. As Linolosi explained, the cattle get diarrhea if kept too long on a rich diet, and ticks and disease build up rapidly in the damp pasture. More importantly, a dry-season reserve that is used year-round would be less useful in a really severe drought. So with Nyiru as a reserve and each group moving a step up the ecological gradient, the Samburu, Rendille, and Turkana were able to keep more animals alive in the drought.

Keeping a herd of animals watered and well enough fed to sustain the people looking after them is a challenge even at the best of times. On the plains of the Sahel, where rainfall is erratic and distances between grazing and water are critical, that challenge created a way of life in which the connection between people and their environment is very direct. Until recent times only a narrow margin separated success from failure. Now, supplementary foods, health care, and the cash economy have broadened the margin. There are more people and more livestock than ever before, despite recurrent drought, famine, and civil strife. The traditional system has expanded to its limits, so people have been obliged to develop other strategies. The sale of livestock, for instance, regularly takes animals from the system. More schools and economic growth foster alternative skills and create jobs that take people from the system, too. As ever in African affairs, the story of the Sahel is one of adaptation to circumstance.

The Sahel sweeps imperiously across Africa south of the Sahara, from the westernmost cape of Senegal on the Atlantic coast to the ramparts of the Ethiopian massif, then south and east across southern Ethiopia, northern Kenya, and Somalia to the Horn of Africa—the continent's easternmost point. It is a 4,300-mile ribbon of unbroken savanna, never less than 185 miles wide. Sahel is an Arabic word meaning "shore"—the shore of the Sahara Desert. Like a high-water mark that advances and retreats with the tides, the Sahel has moved north and south with the climatic changes that have affected the Sahara over the millennia, but has always been an unbroken east-west corridor across Africa.

The region hosts an impressive variety of cultures and languages—the Fulani of Senegal and Mali, the Peul of Niger, the Dinka of Sudan, and the Samburu of Kenya, to name a few. But although the differences among these groups may seem significant, they reinforce more than they disguise the overriding importance of the one thing they all have in common. All are herders, and most are cattle herders. The ability of the cow to convert grass into food has inspired people to exploit resources that otherwise would have been unusable. It could be said, in fact, that the cow has underwritten the history of the Sahel.

All domestic cattle are descended from the wild aurochs, *Bos primigenius*, that once lived in southwest Asia and southeast Europe. Thus they are of temperate origin, and thrive best in temperate regions. In the Sahel, however, cattle confront conditions that are both very hot and very dry. Water is critical, and they need to pass huge volumes of water through their systems in order to keep cool. Selective breeding has produced cattle that can go without water for a few days, but water deprivation puts a significant strain on them. They rapidly lose condition. And for pastoralists on the Sahel, keeping their herds in good condition is crucial—their lives depend upon it.

Every aspect of the pastoralist lifestyle is determined by the environment. Wide variations in annual rainfall mean the pastoralists must always raise as many animals as possible, for next year it might not rain at all. This determination to maintain large herds is often criticized on the assumption that livestock is regarded as a form of wealth and that large herds are a sign of avarice, but this is wrong. A large number of livestock represents insurance in case of disaster. Lepusiki had 200 cattle when the 1984-85

Okra, picked here in a Diafarabé garden, is a native African plant. Also known as lady's fingers, or gumbo, it features in tropical dishes. It can be boiled, fried, dried, or pickled, or used to thicken stews.

drought set in. He lost 80 percent of them, but still had 40 animals to feed his family when the drought broke. Had he started out with 40 (a number the agroeconomists might recommend) and lost 80 percent, Lepusiki and his family would have found it impossible to survive and rebuild the herd from the remaining 8 animals.

Goats and sheep are another important aspect of the pastoralists' survival strategy that is often criticized. Goats are especially denigrated because they are said to breed too fast and degrade the environment. But goats are a vital safety net—the last to stop giving milk as a drought intensifies and the

first to begin again when rain returns. The Samburu built up large flocks of sheep and goats during the dry years of the 1970s. Many of these animals survived the 1984-85 drought that killed their cattle, and large numbers were subsequently traded for the Ethiopian and Somali cattle with which the Samburu replenished their herds.

Like most Sahelian pastoralists, Lepusiki will sometimes provide meat for his family, and in times of hardship they will drink blood taken from living animals. In modern times, their diet has been supplemented by cereals of various kinds, but milk remains their staple food. The advantages of basing

Farmers on the inland delta of the Niger River plant a succession of crops as the flood rises and falls over their fields—rice on the rising waters, sorghum and millet when the receding flood leaves saturated soils.

their survival on milk rather than on meat are considerable. Milk protein is produced five times more efficiently than meat protein. Milk can be obtained daily, whereas a cow supplies meat only once in its lifetime. Also, milk production resumes within days of a drought breaking, while muscle tissue takes months to regenerate.

But the difficulties of keeping cows well enough nourished to produce offspring—and thus, milk—imposes heavy burdens of responsibility on the men who lead the group. They must have profound knowledge of the landscape and its climatic cycles and of the people who tend their herds. It is not enough to know where there is grass today. They must know where it can be found in the days and months ahead, how long it will sustain how many cows, where there will be sufficient water, and when the herds must be taken to the sparsely distributed salt pans. The leaders must calculate when to leave for fresh pasture, and they must know when calves are due and which cows will come into estrus next.

Samburu society has been described as a gerontocracy—one that reveres its elders. And no wonder. The elders are an indispensable source of knowledge. They know their environment, people, and animals intimately. They monitor the phases of the moon and the movement of the stars and planets to determine the seven seasons of the year when rain might fall.

Beyond what they know of the land and what they can see in the stars, the Samburu believe their fate lies in the hands of their deity, Nkai, whose name also happens to be the Samburu word for "rain." This powerful belief conditions everything they do. The Samburu live in a marginal environment, often at the edge of starvation, and yet where one might expect a hard, intolerant manner, an air of grace prevails. When elders meet, their greetings take the form of questions—asking after the family, the livestock, the land. The replies are always positive, accompanied by a slight bow of the head and the words "Nkai, Nkai" repeated in supplicatory tones. On parting, elders will offer blessings to their juniors, and again the response is "Nkai, Nkai." Children will walk up to newly arrived elders and silently await blessings, to which, once again, the response is "Nkai, Nkai." The name of God and the word for rain are constantly repeated in the community.

Nkai is said to reside in a cave on Mount Nyiru, high above the arid Sahelian plains. Indeed, as a haven from the trials of a scorching drought, Nyiru is close to paradise. The slopes are cloaked with forests, and burbling brooks lace the meadows of the summit plateau. There is honey and wild fruit, and the cattle give rich milk. Nkai—both as God

and rain—has blessed Mount Nyiru, however devastated the land around may be.

West of the Samburu lands in northern Kenya, the Fulani constitute one of the largest cattle-raising peoples in the world. Nearly 16 million strong, the Fulani are unique among all people of Africa in how far they are scattered. In every country from Senegal to Sudan, there are people speaking Fula languages. They have different names in different regions, but they share a common heritage and are known collectively as the Fulani. Only a small fraction are true nomads—people who move constantly and live entirely off the produce of their herds. Most are what has been termed "semisedentary," following a way of life that combines both herding and agriculture.

The semisedentary Fulani have settled villages, often along rivers or near other permanent sources of water. They farm, with millet as the staple crop, and keep large herds of cattle. Unlike the Samburu, whose cattle are herded far and wide during the dry season, the semisedentary Fulani keep their herds at home during the dry season and graze them far afield during the wet.

Sending the cattle away from the village during the wet season leaves the land free for cultivation. The crops are harvested by the time the cattle return, and the stubble provides fodder while the cattle manure the land. Meanwhile, by leaving the village during the wet season, the cattle are able to make use of pastures where water isn't typically available. The milk from the roaming herds does not go to waste, for it feeds the herdsmen and—most crucially of all—feeds and fattens calves that would get much less sustenance if their mothers were being milked in the village. Thus the semi-sedentary Fulani get the best of both worlds during the rainy season: while their farmland is producing its bounty of grain, their herds are gathering the fat of the land.

Generous though the cow has been, its temperate origin makes it susceptible to a terrible disease residing harmlessly in the continent's indigenous wildlife. This is trypanosomiasis—*nagana* in cattle, sleeping sickness in humans. It is caused by single-cell parasites that invade the bloodstream, disarm the immune system, and build up to numbers that the body cannot sustain. If left untreated, the most virulent forms of the disease can kill in weeks; less virulent forms may linger on for years. All attack the central nervous system in their final stages, inducing seizures, delirium, sleepiness, and coma—hence the name, sleeping sickness.

Justin's illness began with a headache and a slight fever, aching joints, and a persistent weariness. A few weeks later, he simply did not want to wake up. He was one of a hundred patients being treated for advanced sleeping sickness in Tambura Hospital in southern Sudan. He was 12 years old, and the doctor could not say that he would live another 24 hours.

Justin had been brought to the hospital five days before. For three days, nurses gave him a drug that had reduced the number of parasites in his body, but Justin had suffered a reaction. Now his brain and spine were awash with dead parasites, and his immune system was frantically attacking the debris and inflaming the surrounding tissue. Justin whimpered as the nurse gave him an injection of steroids. She hoped that by reducing the inflammation, the steroids would ease the pressure on Justin's swollen brain.

The hope was fulfilled. Justin was still alive when the doctor made her rounds the next day. The swelling had gone down, and he was propped up on his elbows. Though he didn't smile or talk to her, the doctor was relieved to find him so much better. It meant he would probably survive.

The microscopic parasites that had taken Justin to death's door were injected into his bloodstream by a fly—the tsetse fly—which in turn had ingested them with the blood it had taken from a wild animal. The tsetse's only source of nourishment is blood. They feed every day, and with a rapierlike proboscis capable of piercing even the hide of a rhinoceros, there are few animals they do not dine upon. People and cattle are inevitably bitten because the preferred habitat of the tsetse is the same as for humans and domestic animals. This habitat amounts to nearly half of all the land in

Cattle are the wealth of the village, sent away to graze the Sahel's wet season flush of grass while crops are raised on the village lands.

sub-Saharan Africa, distributed through 36 countries. At least 50 million people live in these regions, with almost as many cattle.

About 300,000 people are infected with sleeping sickness each year in Africa, and about 20,000 succumb to it. Experts have estimated that without the tsetse fly Africa would be between two and five billion dollars per year better off. Calculations like this have encouraged the World Health Organization, the United Nations Food and Agricultural Organization, the European Union, and others to devote millions of dollars to eradicating the tsetse fly and sleeping sickness. For now, though, treatment of infected individuals and control of the tsetse population offer the best hope of relief.

Paradoxically, bringing in more people and their cattle seems to be the most effective way to control the tsetse fly. Continuous grazing ensures that no tree or shrub seedling grows more than a few inches high, and with tree cover restricted, the tsetse are kept at bay. Where villages are established, people destroy the fly's natural habitat and scare away or kill the fly's wild animal hosts. Thus it has been found that where there are more than 100 persons per square mile, tsetse infestation falls below threatening levels.

As the Nile lays a green ribbon of prosperity through the eastern Sahara, so the Niger River pours life-giving water across a vast swath of the southern Sahara—the Sahel region of Mali. Farmers, fishermen, herders, and hunters have been exploiting the rich environment for thousands of years. At Jenne-jeno, archaeologists are unraveling the evidence of a unique history: broken pottery, clay net weights, spinning whorls, grindstones, cooking fires. A wall of the excavation trench reveals 1,600 years of continuous occupation, and the descendants of these people are here still.

The Niger River rises from a highland massif in Guinea, near the border of Sierra Leone. Although the source is little more than 150 miles from the Atlantic Ocean, the river flows inland and, supplemented by its tributaries, takes a grand, circuitous route to the ocean: northeast through the Sahel to Timbuktu, then curving east and southeast across Niger and through Nigeria to its estuary on the Gulf of Guinea. It covers a distance of 2,600 miles.

The highlands and the adjacent Tingi Mountains in Sierra Leone are among the world's most ancient, and when they were heaved from the Earth's primeval mass, about 3.6 billion years ago, their rocks were laced with veins of mineral ores. Over millions of years, erosion stripped huge amounts of rock from the ancient formations, washing away the mineral residues. As a result, iron and aluminum ores are commonplace throughout the region, along with rich deposits of gold and diamonds.

Sedimentary sands and clays have accumulated to the north of the mountains in such quantities that their weight has caused the underlying basin floor to subside. This feature is familiar to geologists as the Taoudenni Syncline and is one of the largest of its kind in the world. Where the Niger River flows across it, the Taoudenni Syncline is notable for its sandstone outcrops and escarpments, its elevated riverbanks, and its expanses of gentle undulation. The land's diversity belies an underlying uniformity.

In effect, the sediments filling the basin have settled like sugar in a bowl. Over its total expanse the surface is remarkably level. Where the Niger veers northeast around the Bandiagara Plateau, the river drops just 32 feet over a distance of more than 125 miles and spreads in a tangle of meandering streams that shift their course with the annual flood. But they are always reunited near Timbuktu, where the Niger becomes a single course once again.

Like the Nile, the Niger is powered by high seasonal rainfall in the mountains. With the onset of the rains, the river swells substantially, rushing toward the basin. Here the meandering streams soon fill to overflowing and steadily inundate the flat, dry land. In a year of average rainfall, the flood transforms nearly 12,000 square miles of parched Sahel into an intricate lattice of channels, ponds, marshes, and lakes. Interspersed are tracts of dry land on which houses are packed tightly together. This is the inland Niger Delta.

The flood begins to rise in September, but the waters take time to reach the most distant and elevated parts of the delta. These parts are flooded for only a month or two. The lowest ground, on the other hand, may be submerged for more than six months under ten feet of water. The height of the seasonal flooding is reached in early November, and levels everywhere then begin to fall. By May the delta is so dry again that even the main channels are less than ten yards across and barely knee-deep.

As the flood spreads over the parched delta floodplain, the water is enriched with nutrients released from decaying vegetation and the droppings of grazing animals. The nutrients fuel an explosive growth of bacteria, algae, zooplankton, and vegetation. The richness of the inland Niger Delta offers people several ways of making a living. Farmers sow the domesticated West African rice *Oryza glaberrima* on soils wet with summer rains. During the flood they harvest wild rice and the cereal species *Echinochloa* from canoes. As the flood recedes, millet and sorghum are grown on the newly saturated soils.

For pastoralists the retreat of the flood coincides with the advance of the dry season in the Sahel regions they had been exploiting to the north. Their herds graze upon exposed pasture and crop stubble as they draw nearer to their home villages after the long wet-season trek.

A third major way of life, surprising on the verge of the Sahara Desert, is fishing. In the dry season, the delta's fish are either confined to the bed of the river or trapped in small, isolated ponds and swamps on the floodplain. Either way, their numbers are very low. But this changes dramatically with the arrival of the flood.

The flood stimulates the production of enormous quantities of their food: algae, plankton, aquatic plants and insects, even other fish. As the fish disperse through the delta, their numbers increase rapidly. High water is the main season of feeding for nearly all the delta fish species. They grow fast as they build up fat reserves to see them through the dry season ahead. Then, as the flood subsides, the aquatic habitat

OPPOSITE: A corner of a Diafarabé home is where a Fula woman keeps the items she will take to marriage. Mats woven of reeds and palm fronds, embroidered blankets, baskets, dishes, and decorated calabashes—all await her future home.

shrinks. Food supplies dwindle and a mass exodus begins.

The large carnivorous fish are the first to move downstream, lurking at the exits of channels through which the abundant young-of-the-year must pass. Shoals of fish are stranded in the rapidly shrinking pools on the floodplain, where food and cover are limited and mortality high. This is the main fishing season for birds and people. Huge quantities of fish are taken year after year, but the inland Niger Delta fishery survives because only ten percent of the juveniles are needed to sustain the breeding population.

Herders, farmers, and fishermen began making intensive use of the inland Niger Delta about 4,000 years ago, probably as the Sahara dried out and forced its inhabitants to migrate southward. Farmers made iron tools and began cultivating the wild West African rice, which became a crucial element of their remarkably stable lifestyle.

Wild West African rice was very likely domesticated in the delta and has successfully held off the diffusion of the higher-yielding Asian varieties, largely because of its capacity to produce a crop under a wide range of conditions. More than 41 distinct varieties of *O. glaberrima* are known, some of which will grow in as much as 9 feet

of water (3 feet is the maximum for Asian rice). The delta's rice farmers sow a mixture of varieties in the same field, each with different growing periods. They also make multiple sowings at intervals of days or weeks in fields that cut across several soil types. These complex procedures enable farmers to produce as much rice as possible from every scrap of available land. The procedures and timing of this rice cultivation are subject to a number of considerations—including cosmological observations—and constitute a body of specialized knowledge that passes from generation to generation but is not readily shared with outsiders.

Specialized knowledge is also fundamental to the procedures by which the herders and fishermen get the best returns from their use of the delta, and with each group usually producing surpluses, trade brought the groups into close proximity—especially when the delta was flooded and living space limited. Once population densities had reached a critical point, the different groups often used the same piece of land at the same time, and the potential for strife was considerable. The inland Niger Delta might have been a morass of hostility. But what distinguishes the early history of people in the delta is not frequent conflict, but a total lack of it.

The history of Jenne-jeno, for example, appears to have been extraordinarily peaceful. While evidence of dwellings destroyed by fire is common at urban archaeological

Rice and cattle are two mainstays of life along the Niger River. Fish is the third. From canoes and across the floodplain, prodigious quantities of fish are taken from the river.

sites elsewhere, not a whiff of such occurrences is evident at Jenne-jeno. The reason for this is principally environmental. Although the inland Niger Delta is a well-watered paradise for a few months of the year, it is still part of the Sahel. And so when the floodwater has evaporated, soaked into the ground, or flowed on downriver, the people of the delta are dependent upon whatever the Sahel has to offer. Like Lepusiki in Kenya, surviving the bad times is what matters. The true history of the Sahel is an account of grueling battles against the environment, not people. And it is a hard and unforgiving environment, one that rewards cooperation, not conflict.

Diafarabé, on the banks of the Niger River in Mali, is abuzz with excitement. The cattle and the young Fulani herdsmen are returning at last—after eight long months. Across the river the cattle are plunging into the water. The herdsmen swim alongside, urging the snorting, floundering beasts forward. All emerge joyfully on the Diafarabé shore—the men laughing, the cattle fat and sleek. This moment is the climax of the year. The future of the community is secure.

Numbering nearly 16 million, the Fulani are probably the largest group of pastoralists in the world today. With their traditional way of life dominating the Sahel region, they are found in every country from the Atlantic to the Nile, united in their descent from people who began herding cattle on the grasslands of the Sahel less than 2,000 years ago. The rigors of herding created the enduring nature of Fulani society and culture, while the Sahel enabled the Fulani and their cattle to spread far and wide.

Sahel is the Arabic word for "shore," but this is the shore of a desert—the Sahel marks the southern edge of the Sahara—where there is just enough rain to produce a broad ribbon of sparse bush and grassland. Waterholes are few, and although the Sahel range is huge, the grazing is spread thin. But each generation of Fulani herdsmen learns how to reap the distant harvest.

Errou is nearly home. He and his companions have brought the cattle safely to the banks of the Niger River after a long and arduous trek through the Sahelian grasslands. "It's a tough job," he says. "We walk from sunrise to sunset. We get very thirsty, and the cows get tired. You constantly have to find new grazing. That's what's always in your head. In the bush you have to be completely focused...your mission is to bring back fat cattle."

gre

at Lakes

Born of the upheavals that created the Great Rift Valley, the Great Lakes stand high in world rankings of significance and spectacle. Lake Victoria is the world's second largest freshwater lake. Lake Tanganyika is so deep that it holds one-hundredth of all the world's freshwater—enough to inundate all of North America.

The region's rainfall is abundant, its soils are fertile, and the climate is warm. Of all Africa, the environs of the Great Lakes are the most richly endowed with the combination of land and climate that fosters the growth of human populations. Bantu farmers first settled here 3,000 years ago. Their numbers grew steadily, multiplying with the introduction of the banana, maize, and cassava.

Rwanda, Burundi, and western Uganda constitute the most densely populated region on the continent—Africa's Garden of Eden. But as the tragic history of the region has revealed, there are serpents in the garden.

Lake Kivu lies on the border of Congo and Rwanda in Africa's Garden of Eden. *FOLLOWING PAGES:* The Equator crosses Lake Victoria at Entebbe, Uganda, the site of this weekly market. Farmers here can produce all year round.

Seated comfortably in the shade of orange trees, with the child on his knee eating a banana freshly plucked from the grove behind the house, Mr. Maneke announced that yes, he would be happy to spend a few days explaining the ins and outs of agriculture on Ukara, an island lying off the southeastern shore of Lake Victoria. Though only 30 square miles in area, Ukara has supported a population of no less than 16,000 people ever since they were first counted more

than a century ago. That gives the island an average population density of 530 per square mile, nearly 6 times that of Tanzania as a whole. Clearly, the farmers of Ukara must be doing something right.

With so little room for expansion, intensified production was the secret, Mr. Maneke explained. Every available scrap of cultivable land was used to maximum advantage. Irrigation and terracing kept land lying close to the island's streams in continuous production. The lakeshores, where the danger of flooding was a threat to food crops, had been dug out and converted to water meadows, providing a steady harvest of grass for livestock.

Mr. Maneke himself had five cattle, and was keen that I should see them. I expected to be taken to grazing land but instead found that the animals spend their lives in shallow circular pits, with a low surrounding fence and a thatched roof, and they seemed healthy and content. They were watered and fed regularly, and the manure accumulating in the pit was cleared out every six months or so and spread on the millet, maize, and cassava fields.

Abundant water and fertile soils rarely occur together in Africa, but the heart of the

A little egret fishes on Lake Victoria. Though a relatively young lake, more than 400 species of fish evolved here.

continent is different. Here the shudders of earthquakes and volcanoes that rippled down the Great Rift Valley 20 to 30 million years ago left a string of lakes and the makings of fertile volcanic soils. The Equator crosses Africa at this point, but since no part of the region is less than 3,200 feet above sea level and much of it stands above 6,500 feet, conditions are never as hot and humid as in the equatorial lowlands. Furthermore, the elevated landmass draws in moisture-laden winds and so receives dependable rainfall. According to locality, rainfall is relatively high and equably distributed throughout the year. Even the two short dry seasons rarely are without rain.

Verdant hills soak up the rain, and streams and rivers carry the off-flow down into some of the world's most exceptional freshwater lakes. Only Russia's Lake Baikal is deeper than Lake Tanganyika, and only North America's Lake Superior is larger than Lake Victoria. Lake Kivu fills the spectacular green encircling the crater basin of a long-dead volcano in the Virunga Mountains; Lake Edward lies in the shadow of the legendary Mountains of the Moon; Lake Albert channels the waters draining from the highlands of the eastern Congo into the Nile.

Of all Africa, the Great Lakes region is most richly endowed with the resources that encourage people to settle. Banana

groves stand tightly packed; the maize does well; the cattle supply milk, manure, and meat as well as bullocks to pull the plow; a small plantation of coffee trees brings in cash for the purchase of household essentials. The land-use system in the Great Lakes region in fact is capable of supporting ten times more people per square mile than Mozambique, for instance. Burundi has 87 percent of its land area under permanent cultivation and pasture—more than any other country in the world.

It is no accident, then, that the countries of this region—Rwanda, Burundi, and western Uganda—are the most densely populated in Africa. But as the world knows, the 1990s laid a pall of unspeakable cruelty and slaughter over Africa's most bountiful landscape: genocide.

This most horrifying episode had its roots in Europe's ideas of racial superiority, which persuaded colonial administrators to patronize the cattle-herding Tutsi even though the Hutu farmers were about eight times more numerous. The Hutu and the Tutsi shared a common origin and language, but the cattle culture of the Tutsi, with its haughty conceits and apparent dedication to the accumulation of wealth, gave these pastoralists an aristocratic demeanor with which the German colonial administrators readily identified and upon which the Tutsi were only too keen to capitalize. They told the colonizers they owned all the region's land and cattle and that the country was ruled by Tutsi princes. Predictably, the colonizers saw these claims as a means of facilitating German control of the region. They introduced a system of indirect rule, governing the territory according to the Tutsi claims of authority.

This did not augur well for the future. Throughout the period of colonial rule, the Tutsi, who made up only a small minority of the population, tightened their grip on every aspect of social, economic, and political control. But opposition grew as the independence movement gained impetus throughout Africa, and when Rwanda and Burundi became independent in 1962, the majority—Hutu—emerged victorious. In the interests of peace, the new Hutu government might have been expected to advocate reconciliation and appeal to national pride. In this case, however, nationalism had not been aroused by aims to drive out a colonial regime; it had been inspired by ambitions to take over an oppressive indigenous hegemony that the colonial government had installed and supported. Once in power, the Hutu elite sought not national unity but absolute supremacy.

An official policy of ethnic quotas was introduced. Since the Tutsi made up only nine percent of the population, they were allocated only nine percent of the school places and no more than nine percent of posts in the civil service or any other area of employment. This oppression was reinforced with officially sanctioned physical

The future of a country rests with its children. A generation lost the chance of education during the genocide. But in Uganda at least, the government has made education a priority.

persecution. There were forced migrations, mass exoduses, and killings. Rwanda and Burundi became partners in a terrible dance. Fear and reprisal created a cycle of violence, culminating in the killings of 1994, when at least 800,000 Tutsi and 10,000 Hutu perished. In the space of just 100 days the Tutsi population of Rwanda was reduced from 930,000 to no more than 130,000. The reverberations of fear spread, inciting spasms of killing in neighboring Burundi and the Congo (then Zaire). A massive exodus eventually led to nearly two million people living in refugee camps sponsored by the United Nations in Tanzania. Most have gone home, but the region is still traumatized, and the history of the Tutsi and the Hutu stands as a terrible indictment of the concept of tribalism that the colonial era brought to Africa.

In Zambia, the chief of a little-known group once remarked: "My people were not

the Soli until 1937 when the Bwana D.C. [Mr. District Commissioner] told us we were." Indeed, ethnic thinking was rare in Africa before it was applied by the colonial authorities, who believed that every African belonged to a tribe, just as every European belonged to a nation. These concepts bore little relation to the continent's kaleidoscopic history, but they were the shifting sands upon which colonial administrators imposed a new political geography. Once the process was set in motion, it was reinforced by the Africans themselves. These invented histories seemed to offer hope of more order and certainty in their lives.

And with the tribes came the chiefs. Throughout Africa, tribal identity became the catalyst that enabled ambitious individuals and groups to achieve positions of status, dominance, and wealth. Tribes became the bases from which politicians launched the drive for national independence. Tribes were also an ideological refuge in times of hardship, when tribal sentiment polarized into a sense of "them and us" that too often erupted in bloodshed.

But outsiders also introduced something that ultimately would help sustain this region—namely, the staple foods that would feed its large population. The indigenous African crops, such as sorghum, millet, and yam, offered limited opportunity for exploiting the region's well-watered, fertile soils. The absence of a dry season impeded their growth, their cultivation was very demanding, and they rarely produced more food than could feed the people required to grow them. But the banana and the plantain introduced an entirely new dynamic.

Though the banana that Mr. Maneke had given his son when I called at the homestead was primarily intended to keep the child occupied while we talked, it was also a clue to the fruit's importance as a staple food. Africa produces 35 percent of the world crop, and where bananas and plantains are the staple diet, Africans each eat about 550 pounds per year. Bananas and plantains are an excellent energy food, and they are a good source of potassium and vitamin C. And the value of the banana is not limited to nutrition. The limited amount of labor it demands is equally important, since that enables even small families to produce a regular and dependable supply in large quantities—for food and for sale. Bananas are a perennial crop, and a well-maintained banana grove will produce good crops for 30 years or more.

How and when the edible banana and plantain were brought to Africa from their point of origin in Southeast Asia is still a mystery, but they are known to have been grown in the region for about 2,000 years. Furthermore, Africans have been growing them so intensively since they arrived that the varieties they have developed constitute a larger pool of diversity than anywhere else in the world. Of the banana cultivars grown in the Great Lakes region, for example, 60 are exclusively African. West of the Great Lakes region, the diversity of the plantain is even more impressive: About 120 distinct cultivars have been developed.

The banana can survive a moderate drought but does not fruit if the soil remains dry for more than a short while. So although it is grown throughout much of Africa, it can be relied upon as a year-round staple food crop only in the equatorial conditions of the Great Lakes region, where rainfall is more or less continuous and temperatures are always relatively high.

Overall, bananas and plantains had a tremendous impact on the demography of equatorial Africa. The boost to agricultural productivity lifted population growth rates and increased the size of settlements. But banana production was not the only activity that rose to distinctive heights of achievement in the Great Lakes region. While banana groves became islands of wealth for some farmers, others used the intervening seas of grass as a means of accumulating a more mobile form of wealth: cattle.

The grasslands of the Great Lakes region are among the lushest in Africa. Better watered than the Sahelian savanna yet free of the tsetse fly, they have enabled people to maximize the breeding potential of cattle with little concern for their ability to withstand drought. But the cattle here are not the utilitarian creatures familiar to Western eyes. The most treasured herds on these rich grasslands are bred to be admired more than to be used. And they are magnificent beasts. As I watched a herd approach in the evening light, their sleek coats rippling over well-fleshed bulk, I could only smile and offer the obligatory admiration to the herdsman walking alongside, who veritably glowed with the pride of possession. His herd and his manner helped to explain why the early colonial administrators had so readily granted the herders superior status over their farming neighbors.

Cattle were already established as a major presence in the Great Lakes region by A.D. 1000, and throughout historical times they have been accorded a degree of prestige seemingly out of proportion to their relevance as a source of food. Herding came to be regarded as a noble pursuit, and cattle were objects of adoration. From the basic long-horned and humped zebra stock (Bos indicus), the herders bred for size—of both body and horn. In modern times, horn spreads of over six feet have been noted.

In folk history and legend, cattle were elevated to reverential status, becoming the companions of royal heroes and attendants to the godlike beings of antiquity from

Bananas were first domesticated in Southeast Asia and introduced to Africa about 2,000 years ago. Nowadays Africa produces over one-third of the world crop.

whom the herders believed they were themselves descended. The herders ultimately became rulers whose powers were measured in the size and quality of their herds. Several such herders, in fact, found themselves elevated to the status of kings under British colonial rule.

Buganda, Bunyoro, Ankole, Acholi, Toro—all were identified by the British as native kingdoms, each with a royal lineage. Since Buganda was bigger and more unified than any other group, British control was consolidated by implementing the Buganda model. The country was named Uganda. Colonial headquarters were established in

the Buganda heartland, and the BaGanda were employed as agents of the administration. The institutions of the BaGanda were imposed upon the rest of the population.

As in Rwanda and Burundi, this was a recipe for trouble. The despotic rule of Uganda's first president, Milton Obote, was ended by the military coup that brought Idi Amin to power in January 1971. After a few months of hope, Uganda lost its way again, and violence became endemic. The country endured eight years under one of the most repressive and destructive regimes that Africa has known. The horror ended with nearly three years of full-scale war, which

Introduced to Lake Victoria in the 1950s, the Nile perch has transformed both the lake and its surroundings: Once abundant, the species is now threatened, having eaten much of the lake's indigenous stock.

finally deposed Idi Amin and reinstalled Milton Obote. That step backward in turn sparked a guerrilla war from which the government of Yoweri Museveni emerged to take control of the country in 1986. By then the "Pearl of Africa," as Churchill had once described Uganda, was a shattered and fiscally bankrupt country.

How does any government rebuild a nation after more than 25 years of such turmoil? A realistic assessment of the scale of the problem and massive injections of international aid are vital, but education is fundamental to the process by which wounds will heal. In 1997 over five million children were enrolled at primary school, compared with fewer than three-quarters of a million in 1970. More than 33,000 attended high school, compared with just over 4,000 in 1970. The hope must be that these children will learn that a government that ignores regional inequalities is courting disaster. Meanwhile, another Herculean task confronts the country, as Uganda stands at the forefront of Africa's battle against AIDS.

AIDS in Africa is transmitted heterosexually in over 90 percent of cases, and is most

prevalent among people in their 20s and 30s—the most economically active sector of the population. The World Bank believes that the deaths of highly skilled engineers, miners, civil servants, nurses, and doctors are weakening nations so much that instead of expanding, the economies of some African countries will shrink by up to 25 percent as AIDS tightens its grip.

Women bear the brunt of the African AIDS epidemic, but not just because the virus moves more readily from male to female. Customs such as dry sex, polygamy, wife inheritance, and the widespread condoning of male promiscuity all add to the vulnerability of women. Most tragic is the fact that for many African women, the primary reason for having sex in the first place is simply to have children.

In Africa today, where most countries have no social security or pension schemes and where the instability of national currencies makes personal savings pointless, there has never been a greater need for children, who are expected to take care of their aging parents. But they must be healthy children, free of AIDS. Although it is going to be a long haul, there are signs that Africa is moving in that direction—led by women. Female education and empowerment are the key. Already, studies in AIDS-ridden African countries have shown that fewer girls with high school educations get HIV.

And so there is a glimmer of hope here, lit by the resolute determination and good

sense of women—who have always been the mainstay of African society. While the men seek jobs that will pay for the manufactured necessities of life, many African households depend upon the women to produce food that will nourish the family at home. Even today, 80 percent of the population of Uganda, for instance, lives directly off the land. Even those who have jobs in the cities and towns are likely to have some land in the country with a stand of bananas. Having a few coffee trees can also provide a useful supplementary income. Lake Victoria, too, has become an increasingly valuable source of profit since the 1980s, when international and local developments opened a new world for its fishermen.

Lake Victoria is the largest lake in Africa and the second largest freshwater lake in the world. The waters of the lake are shared by three countries—Tanzania, Uganda, and Kenya—and with a total length of 2,130 miles the shoreline is nearly as long as Africa is broad at the Equator. But statistics alone cannot give any true sense of the lake's formidable presence. It is better to think of it as an ocean—even though the lake lies at the

OPPOSITE: **Brightly colored cichlids are popular aquarium fish. Most are raised in captivity, but breeders will pay good money for genetically pure wild stock. Rare wild species can fetch hundreds of dollars a pair, providing a lucrative occupation for some of Lake Malawi's fishermen.**

very heart of a continent, at an altitude of 3,700 feet above sea level. There is no tide, admittedly, but there are waves slapping a rocky shore and a horizon where the water meets the sky in an unbroken line, curving with the circumference of the Earth.

The lake has sounds, gulfs, and channels of a size that would not disgrace a continental coastline, as well as hundreds of islands. Nonetheless, the lake's expanses of open water are vast. Trawlers wishing to fish in the center of the lake from the port of Mwanza must reckon on a sailing time of close to 18 hours. And the open water is a dangerous place to be when tropical squalls sweep across the lake. Once I spied a capsized canoe, nets and floats entangled with the sodden sail. There can have been little hope for the crew. Even the large modern ships do not risk taking a shortcut across open water.

Lake Victoria is young, geologically speaking. It is located in a basin that was formed 400,000 years ago, when a fractured block of the Earth's crust tilted along the line of the Great Rift Valley, raising its western edge into a range of hills that broke the path of rivers flowing westward until that time. The basin is shallow, and Lake

Dagaa are small but occur in such huge numbers that fishermen sometimes fill the canoe several times in the course of a night.

Victoria is nowhere more than 270 feet deep. Lake Tanganyika, by comparison, boasts a depth of 4,823 feet.

Since the majority of Lake Victoria's annual water budget comes from rainfall, any prolonged decrease in annual rainfall rapidly can lead to falling lake levels. Indeed, the roots and pollen of terrestrial plants found in cores taken from the deepest parts of the lake bed show that the lake has dried out completely three times since its formation, most recently around 17,300 years ago, in the midst of the last major ice age. The lake began to fill again when the climate improved, about 14,700 years ago.

That a body of water slightly smaller than Ireland should dry out and then fill again over such a short period of geological time is startling. People relying on it for sustenance could adapt or move away, but not so the fish. If the lake bed was dry for even a year or two—never mind millennia—no fish could have survived to repopulate the returning waters. Yet modern Lake Victoria has been home to more than 400 species of fish, most of which did not occur anywhere else on Earth. The majority of these are cichlids—the family of tropical freshwater fish often seen in aquariums. They share a common ancestry with fish from rivers and lakes elsewhere in the region, and some of those ancestors must have swum into Lake Victoria as it began to fill again, 14,700 years ago. But their descendents can only have evolved into so many distinct species since that time, making the Lake Victoria cichlids the fastest evolving large group of vertebrate species ever known.

The basic skeletal structure of fish is very adaptable, meaning they can evolve in a relatively short space of time. Reproductive strategies give the cichlids an additional evolutionary edge. While most fish produce a superabundance of eggs and leave their fate to chance, the cichlids lay few eggs and look after them carefully. Nest guarding, egg turning and cleaning, and mouth brooding ensure the survival of a very high proportion of young fish and enable the cichlids to breed all year round. Under favorable conditions, then, the lake's original cichlids increased rapidly.

The 33 genera of cichlids endemic to nearby Lake Tanganyika have evolved ways of exploiting every kind of food source in every available location. There are bottom feeders and surface feeders, plankton eaters and algae eaters, some that live on fish eggs, some that eat fish, and some that must crack open a mussel or break into a snail shell for their meals. But the most amazing feeding specialization of all is that of the *Perissodus* cichlids, whose diet consists only of fish scales taken from living fish. The scale eaters stealthily approach their victims from behind, then suddenly dart in to rasp a mouthful of scales from their sides.

If cichlids have made Lake Tanganyika a unique laboratory for the study of evolution, then the rate at which cichlid species have been exterminated from Lake Victoria makes that lake an illuminating example of how quickly a natural wonder can be destroyed when people become involved. Fifty years ago the cichlids made up more than ninety-nine percent of Lake Victoria's fish biomass; today they account for less than one percent. Many cichlid species are already extinct, and others are so reduced in numbers that their chances of recovery are minimal.

The introduction of the predatory Nile perch in the 1950s has been the major cause of cichlid decline and extinction. But Lake Victoria's problems can be traced back even further, to the 1920s, when large forested areas of the lake's catchment were cleared for tea, coffee, sugar, and cotton plantations. The agricultural activity increased the amounts of soil being washed into the lake—not to mention fertilizer residues and pesticides. Human settlement around the shores added to the pollution. Then came the water hyacinth, *Eichhornia crassipes*, an ornamental plant from South America.

Fed to excess by nutrients from intensified human activities, the tamed water hyacinth of the ornamental pond ran wild.

In a mere 20 years the water hyacinth virtually encircled the 2,130-mile shoreline with an almost impenetrable 100-foot-wide mat of densely packed floating leaves and roots. Concerted attempts by local communities to clear the weed from the lake by hand have been futile. Weevils introduced from South America, where they are the water hyacinth's natural predator, had no impact in Lake Victoria.

Meanwhile, the world price for table fish was rising and transportation costs were falling. By the late 1980s it was possible to make a profit exporting frozen fillets of Nile perch to Europe and the Middle East. By the mid-1990s exports from the Lake Victoria fishery had reached more than 44,000 tons per year. Local trade probably accounted for at least another 5,500 tons. The off-take is huge and this, combined with habitat destruction, population growth, and pollution, has transformed Lake Victoria from a natural wonder into one of the most disrupted ecosystems ever observed.

But the news from Lake Victoria is not all bad. Certainly the millions of people who feed their families either directly or indirectly from the lake have a more positive view of events. And even within the lake itself there have been positive developments.

My visit to Ukara occurred at the time of the new moon, and each evening the lake sparkled with dozens of lights. Fishermen. Mr. Maneke explained that they were after *dagaa,* fish that swarmed to the lights on moonless nights and could be netted by the ton. The catches were so large, he claimed, that some canoes came ashore to unload two or three times during the night. The story seemed improbable, but I was obliged to revise my opinion the next day, when the island tour brought us to the fishermen's beach. An area the size of a railway platform was strewn with these silvery slices of protein, drying in the sun. Much of the previous night's catch was already bagged up and awaiting shipment to the mainland, where a good price was anticipated. The market for dagaa had expanded enormously in the past few years, Mr. Maneke explained, probably because the fish was so much easier to handle and the lake seemed to be full of it at the moment. Why? Mr. Maneke shrugged. Because Lake Victoria is a wonderful place, he suggested.

Dagaa is the local name for *Rastrineobola argentea* which, unlike the cichlids, grows fast, reproduces prolifically, and has a short natural life span. Such fast turnover rates make it exceptionally resilient to predation, whether by Nile perch or by fishermen. From Lake Victoria dagaa is sold throughout East Africa—even making its way to the markets of Tanga, on the Indian Ocean coast. In Kenya and Uganda, an increasing proportion of the catch is turned into a fishmeal animal feed, some of which is fed to

The sun sets behind the rounded volcanic peaks of the Virunga Mountains at Lake Edward, Uganda.
Africa's heartland is a spectacular combination of fertile highlands and exceptional freshwater lakes.

tilapia in commercial fish farms. By the mid-1990s, the dagaa fishery was second only to Nile perch in economic importance on Lake Victoria. With dagaa, Nile perch, and tilapia, the lake had essentially become a three-species fishery. But the combined catches total an estimated 550,000 tons per year, and some fear that the lake cannot sustain such a huge outtake.

Yet Lake Victoria may have more surprises in store. It has been found, for instance, that 13 species of mud-feeding cichlids wiped out by the Nile perch have been replaced by massive populations of a single species of freshwater prawn—on which Nile perch are now growing to the size of small goats. As Mr. Maneke suggested, Lake Victoria is a wonderful place.

Charles Tinkewimenu was born and brought up on a farm. He had not seen Lake Victoria until he visited it as a student, and did not think of working there until he heard of huge profits being made from fishing. "My first time on a boat was very scary, even though I was 30 years old," he admits. "But I had to be strong. I was determined to make a living from fish." Soon he owned several canoes and had crews working for him.

C harles Tinkewimenu has a problem. The fishing in Lake Victoria is not what it used to be. Catches have fallen, and there are more fishermen than ever on the lake. Ten years ago he sold three cows to buy a canoe and the nets he needed to get started as a fisherman, leaving his wife to manage their successful farm. A contract to supply the international animal feed industry enabled Charles to buy more canoes and hire more men. Business boomed. But not anymore.

Lake Victoria is nearly the size of Ireland, but not as permanent as it looks. The lake bed was grassland 15,000 years ago, when the last major ice age locked much of the Earth's water in the ice caps. As the lake basin refilled, it became a hothouse of evolution for fish. Over four hundred species evolved. For centuries, the fishing on the lake was good. And it was even better when fishermen began catching the Nile perch introduced in the 1950s. Then the balance shifted. Having eaten many of the lake's fish species to extinction, the Nile perch itself was in trouble.

But Charles is an enterprising man. He plowed his fishing profits back into the farm, and the farm flourished. Now he will use farming profits to move into a new and growing business—tourism. He is buying a large motor launch that will ferry tourists to the chimpanzee sanctuary that has been opened on Ngamba Island.

coast

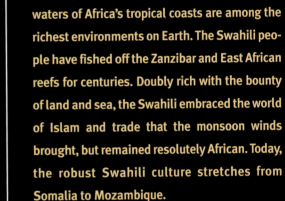

The reefs that lie in the turquoise and azure waters of Africa's tropical coasts are among the richest environments on Earth. The Swahili people have fished off the Zanzibar and East African reefs for centuries. Doubly rich with the bounty of land and sea, the Swahili embraced the world of Islam and trade that the monsoon winds brought, but remained resolutely African. Today, the robust Swahili culture stretches from Somalia to Mozambique.

The Swahili coast was the first part of Africa south of the Sahara touched by the outside world. Dhows from the Red Sea, Arabia, and India were trading with Zanzibar more than 1,000 years before the first Portuguese anchored caravels off the shores of West Africa.

Wherever the foreigners could find safe anchorage, they took away shiploads of Africa's wealth. Millions of slaves were shipped across the Atlantic from West Africa. Millions were shipped from Zanzibar and East Africa, too, where the trade began earlier and went on longer.

The tide rises near Bwejuu, on Zanzibar's eastern shore. *FOLLOWING PAGES:* The culture of East Africa's Swahili coast is a vibrant mixture of indigenous African culture and exotic influence.

Not so long ago, when it was still possible to travel in Sierra Leone with reasonable safety, I took the *pampa* that sailed twice a week across Yawri Bay from Tombo to Shenge. Distance 25 miles, journey time 3 hours. The pampa is a 59-foot open boat locally built of rough-hewn boards. It leaked. And with a 40-horsepower outboard engine driving it into a moderate swell and onshore breeze, it also took water over the bow and starboard gunwale.

The pampa occasionally flushed a flying fish from the cloudy waters of the shallow bay, but there was little to see by the time we were an hour from Tombo. The bulk of the Freetown peninsula was visible to the north, but to the south and east the coast was low and gray, like the first wash of a watercolor—an image so insubstantial that it might have been a cloud bank.

On Africa's coasts, long sandy beaches predominate. Rugged cliffs are rare, and few shores have a backdrop of high mountains. Over long distances the coastline is unbroken by any large inlets, and of its major rivers only the Congo has an open estuary. The rest are either blocked by sandbars or reach the ocean via the twisting channels of a delta. Africa's largely impenetrable coastline helped to deter foreign invaders, while the paucity of protected natural harbors and navigable rivers hindered the development of the coast and its hinterland. Nonetheless, there were a few places where ships could anchor safely, and most of these were at some time or another used by vessels engaged in the African slave trade. Sir John Hawkins anchored in Yawri Bay in 1562, taking on board the cargo that would constitute the first shipment of slaves to be transported across the Atlantic to America.

Toward evening, as the sight of coconut palms and huts confirmed that Shenge was

At sunrise and low tide, fishermen from Bwejuu pole their boats across the shallow waters of the lagoon. The fishing is best off the reef, which lies a good distance offshore, but catches are faltering.

near, a flotilla of outrigger canoes sailed into view: twenty-seven of them, spritsail rigged, each sail a random homemade patchwork of flamboyant cloth. All colors of the rainbow were there, as they might be in Montego Bay when vacationing wind-surfers are out in force. But the men from Shenge were going out for the night, catching their livelihood in the deep blue water that lies five miles offshore. Their course took the canoes close to Plantain Island, where slave traders had built a pen in which to hold their merchandise.

Ben Caulker showed me around Plantain Island the next day. A teacher whose family has lived in Shenge for generations, Ben had

plans to make a tourist venue of the region. Tasteful and low-key, he explained, where visitors could absorb the natural beauty, cultural heritage, and history of Shenge and Plantain Island. Tourists would of course visit the slave pen, which still stands at the northern end of the island—a square of stout stone walls, open to the skies. A path hewn through the boulders leads down to a jetty, pointing west, where the sun sets and ships disappeared into the ocean.

The shipping of slaves across the Atlantic from the shores of West Africa is deeply

etched into the conscience of the world. Less well-known is the trade from ports on the East African coast, which began earlier, went on longer, and at times equaled the Atlantic trade in its volume and depravity. Zanzibar was a center for the marketing and shipment of East African slaves to Arabia and across the Indian Ocean for more than a thousand years—a history that stands in stark contrast to its modern role as an exotic spice-island paradise for tourists.

The canoes with colorful sails that dart across the Zanzibar lagoons evoke memories of the Yawri Bay flotilla. Known as *ngalaus* in the coastal Swahili language, their crews have brought fish from the offshore waters for centuries. But nowadays the Zanzibar canoes are more often filled with tourists, variously attired in sun hats, T-shirts, flippers, snorkels, and masks, sailing out for a glimpse of life on the coral reefs that line the offshore rim of the lagoon.

The tourists go out at low tide. Floating on the surface, they have a privileged view of the richest environments on Earth: tropical coral reefs. A single reef may support as many as 3,000 different species of sea creatures. Shoals of small, bright blue damselfish flash through the branches of the antler coral. Butterfly fish move more sedately, each of their many species distinguished by a different pattern of brilliantly colored spots, dots, patches, and stripes.

The reef's surface is packed with sponges, sea urchins, brittle stars, and sea fans. Sea anemones adorn the coral branches, their fronds waving with the current. Sea lilies, bristle worms, and shell-less mollusks are constantly on the move. Moray eels lurk in small caverns, waiting to feed on whatever passes by. Along the edges of the reef drift the colorful parrot fish. With their beaklike mouths, they nip off pieces of coral to extract the living polyps within.

Coral polyps are tiny creatures belonging to a group known as the *Anthozoa*—the "flower animals." With a flurry of tentacles extending from their cylindrical bodies, they do look like a vase of flowers. But these in fact are carnivorous animals with deadly stingers on their waving tentacles, which are constantly taking a meal of microscopic prey from the passing currents. Coral polyps take calcium carbonate from the sea, too, using it to build the delicate protective chambers from which their tentacles can be extended and retracted at will. Each new generation of polyps builds directly upon the chambers of previous generations, so that by now some reefs rise hundreds of feet from the seabed. But only the surface of the reef is alive—like a thin skin covering layer upon layer of empty limestone chambers.

The coral reef is often called the tropical rain forest of the sea, and although no two

OPPOSITE: **The octopus can change color faster than a chameleon. It has eyesight and other senses to rival ours. It pumps blue blood, is jet powered, and can emit smoke screens of ink. It is also a very popular food on the Swahili coast.**

environments could seem more different, they are fundamentally very similar. Both depend upon profuse sunlight and oxygen. The living surface of the coral is bathed in sunlight, just like the leaves in a rain forest canopy, while the waves breaking over the reefs and surging through the coral heads saturate the water with oxygen, like a wind blowing through the treetops. In addition, the dead coral that supports the living surface of the reef serves much the same function as the inert wood of the trees that hold the rain forest canopy aloft. Of course, since all life began in the oceans, the coral reefs are much older. The earliest evidence of rain forest flora dates back a mere 65 million years, while coral reefs were already well established by 200 million years ago.

A grove of coconut palms shades Bwejuu and also gives the villagers an income from the nuts.

Superlatives crop up frequently in even the most serious academic accounts of the tropical reefs. The tiny polyps add a staggering 2.7 billion tons of material to the reefs each year, for instance, and the growth rate of the reef's plants and animals is greater than in any other ecosystem. Fully one-third of all the world's bony fish—8,000 species in all—as well as numerous less mobile creatures live on tropical coral reefs. The density of fish alone is ten times greater than the densities attained in corresponding temperate ecosystems. It is roughly equivalent to keeping a flock of forty sheep permanently on one acre of grassland.

For many years it was believed that the life of a coral reef was a point of equilibrium, wherein the greatest possible diversity of organisms filled every available niche with the greatest possible numbers, and that this balance denoted stability. But studies have shown that coral reefs are actually highly unstable ecosystems in which self-replacement and recovery from disturbances are the norm and actually contribute to diversity. This is because coral communities have evolved in conditions that are subject to unpredictable and radical change. With hurricanes, storms, and changing sea levels and temperatures to contend with, coral reefs have had to be adaptable.

They are not as fragile as was previously thought, but the damage inflicted by the El Niño events and rising ocean temperatures of recent years will take decades to repair. Some reefs may never recover—especially if global climate change is responsible and its effects permanent. Most worrying of all, the threat of coastal erosion could become acute as the ocean steadily gnaws away the reefs that have been building up protective barriers along the coastline, year by year.

The Swahili fishermen whose livelihood these days may depend more upon ferrying tourists than catching fish represent the eastern limit of the Bantu migration that began 5,000 years ago. After consolidating their numbers in the Great Lakes region, the Bantu farmers moved across the dry savannas to the eastern equatorial coast, where warm currents and easterly winds prevail. As the warm, wet sea air meets the land, it rises, cools, and sheds moisture, which in turn sustains vegetation of extraordinary diversity.

The coastal settlers were also blessed with the bounty of the sea, and boats and inshore fishing have become integral to Swahili culture. But the sea brought the benefit and the tragedy of foreign influence as well. Evidence of East Africa's trading links with foreign parts abounds. Parts of the Swahili coast are littered with sherds of early Chinese ceramics. Iranian pottery dating back to the fifth century has been excavated from sites lying thirty miles inland. Silver coins were in use on the Lamu Archipelago by the ninth century and probably were minted there. Coins from Sicily dated A.D. 1000 give an indication of how far afield the Swahili trade connections had reached.

Wind and current brought these traders to eastern Africa's Swahili coast. Monsoon winds blow constantly here; their direction, like the seasons, is affected by Earth's orbit around the sun. The winds blow steadily from the northeast during the northern winter, then swing 180 degrees to blow from the southwest during the northern summer. The winds are constant, and their speed of 9 to 18 miles per hour is enhanced by the fact that the currents sweeping along the East African coast change direction too.

It was the northeast monsoon that for centuries brought foreign merchants to the Swahili coast. Roman vessels sailed here from Egypt's Red Sea coast in the first centuries A.D., as did Arabian, Persian, and Indian dhows. Chinese documents from the 12th century show that Chinese mariners were familiar with the towns of the Swahili coast by that date. They also knew of snow-capped Kilimanjaro, Lake Victoria, and the Mountains of the Moon—and this was 500 years before Europeans had even the vaguest idea of Africa's hinterland. Chinese connections with Africa were so far advanced that in October 1415, a giraffe arrived in Peking. It had come from Malindi, on the Swahili coast, and the emperor himself received the animal at the gate of the inner palace.

After Aksum in the Ethiopian highlands, the Swahili coast was the first region of sub-Saharan Africa to establish trading links with foreign lands. The Swahili people built trading centers at Lamu, Malindi, Tanga,

Dhows from India, Arabia, and the Red Sea have been sailing to Zanzibar and the Swahili coast on the northeast monsoon for centuries. They brought in luxury goods and took away ivory, spices, and slaves.

Shanga, Zanzibar, Kilwa, and numerous other places along the coast. They traded African produce for foreign goods and developed a distinctive urban society and culture in the process. The most enduring foreign import, though, was the Muslim faith, as shown by a small mosque built at Shanga in the eighth century.

The extent of Islamic influence in Swahili culture has inspired considerable debate as to which predominates. Was the Swahili coast merely the edge of the Islamic world, or was it the center of a significant African world? Increasingly, the evidence indicates that the latter was the case. The history of the Swahili demonstrates the resilience of an indigenous system. At the coast, they took on the world and grew stronger. Their language was enriched by the adoption of Arabic words and idioms for which there was no Swahili equivalent, but it remained a distinctly Bantu language and eventually became the lingua franca of people from the coast to the Congo Basin. Today, Swahili is probably the most widely spoken language south of the Sahara.

The architectural style of buildings on the Swahili coast was also largely indigenous. Stone structures in general and grand buildings in particular—such as the 14th-

A stevedore works in Zanzibar docks, where the import and export of goods relies on manual labor. The island was self-supporting in food until the early 1800s, when clove plantations were established.

century palace and commercial center of Husuni Kubwa—were influenced by a foreign style, but stone buildings were in fact part of a larger complex in which most buildings were made of wood, mud, and thatch. At Kilwa, for instance, the urban site covers about 70 acres but has only a scattering of stone buildings. Many of the nearly 200 sites that have been excavated along the coast are similar. Clearly, stone buildings were merely part of an overall settlement pattern, not the major feature of trading cities established by foreign merchants.

"Kilwa is one of the most beautiful and well-constructed towns in the world," the traveler and scholar Ibn Battutah wrote following his visit to the Swahili coast in 1331. Vasco da Gama was equally impressed when he dropped anchor in the harbor of Moçambique on March 2, 1498. Large dhows were anchored there, manned by Arabs and far better equipped than the Portuguese caravels. Vasco da Gama and his men were greeted by Swahili merchants dressed in rich linens and cottons with silk borders embroidered in gold. The Portuguese were impoverished by comparison, and a dignitary who visited the ships dismissed with contempt the hats, corals, and sundry items he was offered as gifts.

Vasco da Gama returned to the Swahili coast five years later, his ships heavily armed. He sailed into the harbors of Swahili towns demanding submission to the rule of Portugal and the payment of large annual tributes. Towns that refused were attacked, their possessions seized, and protestors killed. Zanzibar was the first to be taken (in 1503). Malindi formed an alliance with the Portuguese, which hastened the fall of Mombasa in 1505; Kilwa was taken in the same year, as were several other towns.

The Portuguese justified their actions as battles in the Christian war against Islam, but there was a powerful mercenary motive, too. A base on the Indian Ocean gave the Portuguese access to the spice trade that otherwise reached Europe only via the Islamic Middle East. Also, as ever, there were rumors of gold in the Swahili hinterland.

The Swahili coast was just one part of a vast Portuguese empire that, at its height in the 16th century, stretched from the Swahili coast to South America to the Spice Islands of the Far East. But the cost of running the empire far exceeded the returns, imposing a drain on manpower and resources that this small, largely agrarian nation could not sustain. The empire eventually collapsed, and the Swahili forts were abandoned.

Meanwhile, the Swahili continued to supply a wide range of goods for local use, for the export trade, and for trade with the interior. It was particularly important to maintain the supply of goods for the interior, for it was from that direction that the Swahili obtained their most valuable export commodities: ivory and slaves.

In 1795 the Scottish explorer Mungo Park traveled with a slave merchant from the western corner of present-day Niger to the Atlantic coast. The merchant had just a few slaves, the last of a much larger contingent captured north of the Niger River. Some had been sold to Tuareg nomads, and some had been sold at markets en route. The remainder were destined for America. Progress to the coast, however, was painfully slow. The slaves were fettered in pairs, Park reports, the left leg of one chained to the right leg of another. They were also tied together in groups of four, with a rope of twisted thongs around their necks.

But despite the agonies of the march, Park found that it was the end of the journey that the slaves feared most. They believed "that the whites purchased Negroes for the purpose of devouring them, or of selling them to others that they may be devoured hereafter, [which] naturally makes the slaves contemplate a journey toward the coast with great terror."

Few parts of Africa were untouched by the slave trade during the centuries of its existence. Some scholars believe that the impact of the slave trade was spread so thinly through the centuries and across Africa that its impact on society as a whole must have been slight. Others contend that the trade transformed human relations within the continent. I agree with the latter argument, simply because the effects of this forced migration were unrelenting and went on for more than 1,000 years. The tragedy of the enslaved was compounded by the turmoil of those who had seen them go. Even the smallest settlement was touched, often more than once. A scattered community of 1,000 people living in the distant interior, for instance, probably had between 6 and 10 of their neighbors and kin abducted every year. This may not seem excessive, considering that disease and other natural causes probably accounted for the deaths of some 50 people per 1,000 each year. But enslavement was more than a natural risk; it was an ever present threat, a fear at the back of the mind, which burdened society with a lingering fatalism as it passed from generation to generation.

Apart from its social effects, the slave trade also had a disastrous effect on the economic development of Africa. The shipping of 9 million slaves across the Atlantic actually required the capture of an estimated 21 million Africans, of whom 7 million were taken into domestic slavery. The remaining 12 million died within a year of capture. Thus the population of much of sub-Saharan Africa did not increase at all, and the continent was denied the economic contribution of those additional millions.

Furthermore, the slave trade shackled Africa to the commercial and political ambitions of Europe, creating an economic system that diverted resources from inland locales toward the coast, where their exchange for European goods represented a net loss to the continent. Textiles, for instance, constituted at least 50 percent of African imports, which stimulated the growth of Europe's textile industry while inhibiting production in Africa. Similarly, the African market for metal goods contributed to the development of mass-production methods in Europe; the low unit costs in turn eliminated any incentive for developing such enterprises in Africa. Even the export of beeswax had a detrimental effect, since gatherers flushed out the bees with fire and responded to high demands by seeking more nests to destroy rather than by adopting sustainable methods.

The item of trade that did the most to keep the slave trade going was firearms. "The natives nowadays no longer occupy themselves with the search for gold," a trader wrote in 1704, "but rather make war on each other to furnish slaves." British traders alone shipped an average of 338,000 guns per year to West Africa between 1750 and 1807; estimates put the total of guns traded at not less than 20 million. The import of firearms into Africa fueled the slave trade and significantly influenced the economic development of the continent thereafter.

The abolition of the slave trade began in the first decades of the 19th century. Yet while abolition first slowed, then finally halted the export of slaves, inside Africa it merely shifted enslavement from one area of economic activity to another: 300 years of trading had created a brutally efficient system that could not be easily stopped. Without a market, the merchandise clogged the system, constituting not only a loss of revenue but also a drain on resources, for slaves had to be fed. The first response to abolition was therefore the most obvious. Slaves were set to work producing food in greater quantities than ever before.

The former slave-trading nations eventually declared that the outlawed slave trade should be replaced by what was called the "legitimate trade." Self-servingly, this trade supplied Europe with raw materials and commodities that were expensive or unobtainable elsewhere, such as palm oil, ivory, hardwoods, rubber, beeswax, and gum arabic. African entrepreneurs also were encouraged to grow introduced crops such as groundnuts, sugar, cocoa, tea, cloves, and cinnamon for European markets, as well as coffee and coconuts.

All these activities were labor-intensive, and slaves who previously had been shipped abroad were put to work on the land. In this way the slave trade became an essential part of Africa's economy. Many more people were enslaved in Africa during the 19th century than when the Atlantic trade was at its height during the 17th century. By 1900, for instance, in the Sokoto region of what is now northern Nigeria, there were at least 2.5 million slaves in a population of 10 million, making it probably the second largest slave society ever known. Only the United States, with 3.9 million slaves in 1860, had more slaves than Sokoto in 1900.

Slavery also turned the wheels of commerce along the Swahili coast. Islam condoned slavery, and Swahili merchants did not regard abolition of the Atlantic slave trade as reason to give up their own lucrative trade. Meanwhile, cloves and cinnamon plantations had been established on Zanzibar and its smaller sister island, Pemba. These proved to be the East African equivalent of the West African gold mines and were equally dependent on slaves—not least because mortality rates on the Zanzibar plantations were extremely high.

Zanzibar's spice trade began in the 1820s when Sa'id ibn Sultan ordered farmers to plant two clove trees for every coconut or risk having their land confiscated. Within a few decades there were three and a half million clove trees on the Zanzibar and Pemba islands—one of the most spectacularly successful agricultural ventures in history. Until then, clove production had been a monopoly of the East Indies, but the plantations on Zanzibar gave the Omanis a majority share of the world market.

By 1840, when the Omani capital was transferred to Zanzibar, the island was producing 3,500 tons per year. Before long, Zanzibar accounted for three-quarters of the total world production. Zanzibar's domination of the world clove market continued

The meticulous carving and bold brass work on traditional doors typifies the blend of African and Arabian influences that is found in Zanzibar's oldest quarter—Stone Town.

through to the early years of independence, but the island's increasing dependence on a single crop made its economy very vulnerable. Since the 1964 revolution, clove production and marketing have been handled by a state-run monopoly whose inefficiency has only compounded the problems of competition and falling prices.

Luckily, though, the decline of Zanzibar's clove industry coincided with the rise of its tourist industry. The number of tourists visiting the island increased more than four times between 1985 and 1996 and continues to rise—but not without bringing a new set of problems. Fishermen, long the main source of dietary protein for the island population, have been only too happy to give restaurateurs first choice from their catches, forcing up the price of fish on the local market and hurting the stocks of some species on the reefs. Lobster, highlight of the tourist menu, is heavily overfished. Other species

are also declining to numbers at which they cannot maintain viable populations.

These very serious issues are unlikely to impinge much upon the dining pleasures of tourists. In fact, the development they are most likely to notice is one that is simultaneously good for Zanzibar and bad for tourism: seaweed farming. Increasingly, the long beaches of white sand and turquoise waters are being outfitted with wooden posts and nylon ropes on which cuttings of commercially valuable seaweed are grown. Within two to four weeks, small pieces of seaweed stem grow tenfold and are ready for harvesting. The wet weed is laid out to dry on plaited palm fronds, then packed in sacks for sale to the U.S. and Europe.

With such promising incentives and such minimal requirements for cultivation, it is hardly surprising that seaweed farming has grown on Zanzibar almost as rapidly as does the plant itself. A 1995 survey found 10,000 people directly involved in seaweed production at not less than 19 locations, with another 40,000 people indirectly involved—and those figures have increased significantly since then. The impact of these developments is social as well as economic. Seaweed farming is overwhelmingly a female activity, and its success has given women a degree of financial independence that breaks the mold of gender relations in Zanzibar's devoutly Muslim society.

Whereas women previously were seldom seen in the markets and had no control over the income that their husbands gained from crops they had grown, women in the seaweed business now sell their produce themselves. They keep the income they earn and decide how it should be spent. Some have exercised their rights to divorce by paying back the bride wealth, and others have chosen to marry with the clear understanding that they are financially independent of their husbands.

The shores that encircle Africa have been both a blessing and a curse to the continent. On the one hand, they offered the benefit of access to the abundant resources of both land and sea. On the other, they exposed Africa to the exploitation of rapacious visitors. It was not just manpower that the slave trade shipped from Africa. The contribution that those missing millions would have made to the continent was lost with them. After abolition, the so-called legitimate trade, with its emphasis on the export of raw materials, served Europe and America more than it served Africa. For more than 1,000 years the wealth of Africa was stolen away.

A thousand years of exploitation is not a legacy that can be easily forgotten, but

A trading vessel makes for harbor on the Swahili coast. The triangular lateen sail is perfectly suited to the monsoon winds of the Indian Ocean, enabling vessels to sail closer to the wind.

the wheel is turning. It will be some time before Ben Caulker and his fellow enthusiasts can use the quiet natural beauty of Shenge and the history of Plantain Island to their advantage, but the Zanzibar fishermen with their ngalaus full of tourists and the women harvesting seaweed are examples of humanity's irrepressible will to thrive. A generation of Africans has grown to adulthood in independent Africa. They are less inclined than their parents to blame Africa's woes on the burden of its colonial legacy and more inclined to look for their future within the continent rather than beyond it. As they take the helm, Africa is poised to steer a new course, no longer bound by the legacy of its encircling shores.

Issa Simai makes his living from the fish and the octopus he catches on Zanzibar's coral reefs. Every day he spends up to 7 hours diving to depths of 65 feet, staying down for 3 minutes at a time. It is a punishing occupation, but he devotes his free time to an even more punishing activity—soccer. Issa plays for the Zanzibari Leopards, winners of the island's Southern Cup.

The coral reefs of the tropical seas are among the world's most productive environments—and one of the most useful from a human point of view. People have always been able to catch something to eat on the reef. In modern times the reefs are a tourist venue too, and Issa's catch supplies hotels and restaurants as well as the family kitchen. Right now, though, he and his teammates are diving overtime, catching the octopus and lobster that will pay for the Leopards' tournament trip to the mainland.

Zanzibar is the largest island on East Africa's Swahili coast. Monsoon winds blow steadily onto the coast from the northeast for half the year, then turn about to blow away from it for the other half. For 2,000 years, these powerful winds have carried trading dhows from and back to India, Persia, and Arabia. Since the seventh century, traders' influences have slowly fused with the existing African culture, and a new identity emerged: Swahili.

Issa Simai was born in Bwejuu, a small village on Zanzibar's eastern shore. The oldest of six children, he is the only one still living in Bwejuu. The others left for university and jobs in the city, but Issa decided to become a fisherman, like his father.

Issa was taught by his father, going farther out to sea each day until he was good enough to dive alone for octopus. "The sea is very frightening at first," Issa recalls. "It can take up to six months to get used to it."

southe

RN africa

Southern Africa is the continent's treasure house. Only the Earth's oldest rocks contain its most coveted substances—gold and diamonds. The precious minerals locked in rocks more than three billion years old have made South Africa a Croesus among nations, far richer than any other part of Africa. But such wealth was achieved only at an enormous cost to humanity.

For more than a century, Africans labored to produce the wealth—and were paid a pittance for their efforts. Laws hardened the prejudices of white settlers and immigrants, making second-class citizens of indigenous people.

With the release of Nelson Mandela and the fall of apartheid, South Africa has recovered its dignity. Turning away from the iniquities of white rule, Africa's industry can at last play a role in the affairs of the continent, building hope for the future. The barriers built across South Africa's physical and social landscapes are coming down.

Cape Town was described by Sir Francis Drake as "the fairest Cape...in the whole...of the earth." *FOLLOWING PAGES:* On a roadside at the edge of the Kalahari, passing tourists can buy beadwork and decorated ostrich eggshells from San Bushmen.

t he modern history of southern Africa effectively began on November 7, 1497, when Vasco da Gama's fleet of four ships anchored in a sheltered bay about 90 miles north of present-day Cape Town. Da Gama named the anchorage Sta. Ellena Bay (today it is St. Helena Bay). There was a Khoisan (Bushman) encampment near the shore, and da Gama's logbook provides the earliest surviving account of Europe's first contacts with the indigenous people of southern Africa:

The inhabitants of this country are tawny-coloured [the logbook reports]. Their food is confined to the flesh of seals, whales and gazelles and the roots of herbs. They are dressed in skins and wear sheaths over their virile members. They are armed with poles of olive wood to which a horn, browned in the fire, is attached. Their numerous dogs resemble those of Portugal, and bark like them....the climate is healthy and temperate, and produces good herbage.

From St. Helena Bay, da Gama sailed on, taking a wide sweep around the Cape of Good Hope and heading north to anchor in what is now Mossel Bay. Here too the Portuguese found the country inhabited by

the Khoisan—"swarthy of appearance, like those of Sta. Ellena Bay," and the log goes on to record what must be one of the happiest encounters in the history of exploration:

On Saturday [2 December 1497] there arrived about 200 [Khoisan], large and small, bringing with them about twelve cattle, oxen and cows, and four or five sheep; and when we saw them we went ashore at once. And they at once began to play on four or five flutes, and some of them played high and others played low, harmonising together very well...and they danced.... The Commander ordered the trumpets to be played, and we in the boats danced....When this festivity was ended...we

Fynbos mosses and reeds flourish in a *vlei* on South Africa's Cederberg Mountains. The fynbos region supports an astonishing 8,500 different plant species in its mere 34,700 square miles.

bartered a black ox for three bracelets. We dined off this on Sunday; and it was very fat, and the flesh was as savoury as that of Portugal.

The Cape of Good Hope lies as far south of the Equator as Greece is to the north of it. Early visitors from Europe were quick to note that its Mediterranean climate was ideally suited to growing crops that flourished in regions of summer sunshine and winter rain. Indeed, it was the only part of sub-Saharan Africa that was well suited to European settlement. For this reason, too, the cape was devoid of Bantu farmers, whose millet and sorghum were adapted to the summer rainfall regimes of tropical Africa and not suited to conditions in the cape. But as da Gama had noted, the cape was home to the nomadic Khoisan pastoralists with substantial numbers of cattle and sheep. Their population density was low, but not spread evenly over the landscape, since the practice of seasonal migration grouped them in a limited area at any given time of year. So the early visitors who applauded the abundance of livestock in some places also wrote of the empty lands available for settlement in others.

In the European scheme, however, there was little room for the Khoisan, except as slaves working the land they had once roamed freely. Slaves were the backbone of the agricultural labor force, and as elsewhere on the continent, the cape slaves were never a self-reproducing population. Mortality rates were high, and more slaves were needed constantly—and they often came from the new lands over which the settlers claimed possession. As the settlers moved inland, though, Khoisan resistance hardened, setting off the Bushman Wars, in which any Khoisan community was open to attack. The government told settlers to treat the Khoisan as vermin to be hunted and shot. Slaughter was widespread, even according to official records.

By the late 1800s, the Khoisan had been driven into regions that no settler would want to inhabit: the vast, waterless expanses of the Kalahari Desert. Forced to abandon their herding way of life, the Bushmen, as they became known, rediscovered the hunting and gathering skills of our ancestors. And this was how ethnographers of the day found them—no longer the proud pastoralists who had sold beef and mutton to Vasco da Gama. In the eyes of the ethnographers they were primitive hunter-gatherers still living in the Stone Age.

The tubular flowers of *Erica massonii*, an indigenous plant found in the fynbos, are covered with a film of sap.

The Bushmen now became objects of curiosity and amusement. Life casts were made for museum displays. In at least one instance, a body was skinned and stuffed by a skilled taxidermist, then displayed in a Spanish museum of natural history. Live individuals were exhibited abroad in museums, in vaudeville shows, and at world fairs. But careful observers were beginning to notice aspects of behavior that contradicted the image of savagery. The Bushmen's language, for instance, was extremely complex (and linguistic studies have confirmed that the Khoisan languages are phonetically the world's most complex), their knowledge of the Kalahari environment was astoundingly comprehensive, and their technical skills were sophisticated. These were intelligent people, living in an environment requiring high degrees of skill and ingenuity.

Furthermore, they had painted the walls of rock shelters with striking images of their world. Working only with ocher-based pigments, they juxtaposed form and tone to create paintings that bring the beginnings of modern Western art to mind.

At first, experts refused to believe the extraordinary paintings had been made by the Bushmen, attributing them to foreigners instead. These prejudices persisted until the 1990s, when South Africa's apartheid regime collapsed. Objective science exposed the absurdity of such immigration theories. In some cases, the art is older than the sources it is supposed to derive from.

The collapse of apartheid also brought the 1994 election of a black government and the repeal of laws that had denied the San people (as the Bushmen are now known) access to their lands. Katrina, Kaas, and Feke are three sisters of the Khomeni San, all in their 70s, who suffered the oppression of the former racist regimes. In 1953, they were put on display in London, much as freaks were shown around Europe and the U.S. in Victorian times. When they returned home, they found that their families had been evicted from their lands and their father beaten to death by a policeman in the process. The Khomeni homeland had been given over to cattle ranching, its former occupants told to make a home for themselves in the shantytowns of Cape Town. For 40 years they lived on the fringes of Cape Town's urban economy, spurned by the blacks, objects of curiosity to the whites. But the Khomeni San never forgot, and in the late 1990s they won a landmark court case giving them full rights to the land they consider their own.

The Khomeni San are now going back, and Katrina, Kaas, and Feke were among the first to make a preparatory visit. Their reunion with the land was highly emotional. They chattered excitedly about the traditional ways, about the bounty of this seemingly impoverished land, and about how people could make a living there. They believed that when their time came, they would die there.

But the women did not envisage a complete return to the old ways. They wanted an adequate supply of running water, sanitation, and electricity, and expected to pay for these services by conducting visitors through the newly designated Kgalagadi Transfrontier Park, which is itself a creation of a new and enlightened movement in conservation called the peace parks. Ten parks spanning the nations of southern Africa are planned. The aim is to encourage plains game to resume the migration routes along which they once roamed freely. The peace parks movement is also committed to engage local people in the planning and running of the parks—people like the Khomeni San and their vanguard in the region: the sisters Katrina, Kaas, and Feke.

The Bushman hunters who once awaited the arrival of migrating game occupied the most varied and densely packed area of vegetation on Earth—the *fynbos* (Afrikaans for "fine bush"). Though covering only 34,700 square miles, the fynbos region supports an astonishing 8,500 different plant species.

Nearly 70 percent of the fynbos plants are found nowhere else in the world, and the captivating beauty of some—such as the proteas, ericas, watsonias, gladiolas, and mesembryanthemums—has found its way into flower shops around the world. In botanical textbooks, the tiny Cape Floristic Kingdom is known scientifically as one of the world's six botanical kingdoms—on par with the Boreal Kingdom, which covers almost the entire Northern Hemisphere.

The soils of the fynbos generally consist of coarse grits and sand, and do not contain much in the way of nutrients or organic matter. This is because they are derived from the sandstones, slates, and shales of an ancient continent. But while these ancient rocks have crumbled into soils that make farming a challenging proposition, they have bequeathed Africans with an abundance of mineral wealth: gold and diamonds, platinum, chromium, nickel, and other valuable metals.

Diamonds are crystals of carbon, forming only at depths of 90 miles below the Earth's surface, where the overlying rock exerts immense pressure and temperatures are in the range of 1,800°F to 2,100°F. Most diamonds are more than three billion years old, sparkling with fire from the core of the Earth and brought to the surface with material from the mantle that has occasionally burst through the crust. Gold also forms in the mantle and is concentrated near superheated water under immense pressure, in which state the water dissolves substances normally considered insoluble—such as gold—and deposits them as veins of ore in the fissures of solidifying rocks. And as with diamonds, South Africa is rich in gold. More than half of the gold ever produced in the world has come from its mines.

As if gold and diamonds were not enough, geology has contrived to deposit even greater mineral wealth in South Africa. Two billion years ago, volcanic spasms squeezed material from the mantle up through the crust and forced it to spread horizontally along planes of weakness in the sedimentary layers above. The material solidified, creating a subterranean island 250 miles long and up to 6 miles thick, all of one piece. Called the Bushveld Igneous Complex, this unique geological feature is one of the world's great treasure houses, with enough platinum, gold, chromium, copper, nickel, tin, fluorspar, vanadium, and iron ore to last 1,000 years at current mining rates.

The first hint of South Africa's vast subterranean wealth was found in 1867 on the banks of the Vaal River. A Dutch settler, Schalk van Niekerk, was paying a visit to neighboring farmers when he noticed their children playing with some stones they had found along the river. One in particular

OPPOSITE: **Caves near the Klasies River on South Africa's Tsitsikamma coast have yielded evidence of early human behavior, including fossil remains and sophisticated stone tools—evidence of modern appearance and thinking.**

Lesotho has been supplying labor to South Africa's gold and diamond mines for over a century. Going to the mines is a rite of passage for Sotho men.

caught his eye, different from any stone he had seen before. That stone was indeed a diamond, and it was sold in Cape Town for £500—a fortune in those days. Within three years 5,000 prospectors were sifting through the riverbank gravels.

Before long, prospectors located the mouth of the pipe that had brought the diamonds to the Earth's surface—a patch of arid, scrubby farmland that today is known as Kimberley. Within a few years, miners had transformed the site into the biggest man-made hole the world has ever seen, 985 feet across and 295 feet deep. The Kimberley magnates made millions and were poised to

make yet more as they invested their profits from diamonds in the Transvaal goldfields, which were discovered in the late 1880s.

Because the mining of gold and diamonds is difficult, a large amount of cheap labor was needed. The Kimberley mine had to rustle a workforce out of a precapitalist rural hinterland, but within a year of opening, almost every black society south of the Zambezi was represented in the diamond fields. Before long, the migrant laborers began using the laws of supply and demand to their benefit. They refused to accept long-term contracts with any one employer, and with 5,000 claim holders competing for

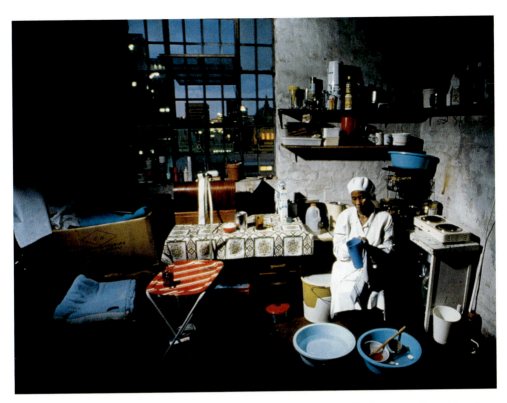

The accommodation provided for South Africa's legions of domestic staff, cleaners, and caretakers is often primitive. In Johannesburg, some live in small shacks built on buildings in which they work.

labor, they moved to whoever was offering the highest wages. Soon labor wages accounted for nearly 90 percent of an average miner's working costs.

But mine owners could not allow laborers to dominate the Kimberley economy. During the 1880s, as Cecil Rhodes moved toward establishing a single monopolistic mining company, De Beers Consolidated Company Limited, the mine managers sought to exercise greater control over the labor force, mainly by requiring laborers to live in company housing. De Beers also used convict labor for free in return for building and running the Kimberley prison.

Although De Beers abandoned the practice of using convict labor in 1932, the gesture was largely academic; the company's compounds were then little better than jails. Once a man entered the compound, he was denied all access to the outside world for the duration of his contract. He moved between the compound and the mine through enclosed passages, and the compounds were roofed over with fine wire netting to prevent stolen diamonds being thrown over the fences.

The Kimberley compounds provided a model for the Transvaal gold mines that came onstream in the 1890s, and together they established a precedent for the management of labor throughout southern Africa. Most workers were migrants living far from home in segregated compounds. Farms, factories, government agencies, and even employers of domestic labor perpetuated the system. Every urban center was surrounded by compounds in which its essential labor was housed—all at a distance from whites.

Segregation and economic exploitation were high among the evils that Africans hoped their independence from colonial rule would redress. After all, many African nations had a healthy economy at the end of the colonial period, helped by a postwar boom in prices—especially the prices of minerals. Copper enriched Zambia. Gold maintained Ghana's buoyant economy. Diamonds enlarged the nest eggs of Botswana, Sierra Leone, and Liberia. Cobalt made the former Belgian Congo a privileged trading partner of the U.S.

The postwar economic boom encouraged Africa's newly independent governments to plan for the future on the assumption that the trend would continue. And real growth did occur. Between 1965 and 1980, sub-Saharan Africa's per capita gross domestic product rose steadily. But 1980 was a turning point, for thereafter sub-Saharan Africa's growth rate fell into a spiral of decline.

By the year 2000, African countries filled all the bottom places in the world tables on health, life expectancy, education, economic status, political stability, and development potential. According to the World Bank, only 15 percent of Africans were living in "an environment considered minimally adequate for sustainable growth and development." A minimum of forty-five percent lived in poverty, one in three were chronically undernourished, and two-thirds did not have access to clean water. One-third was constantly exposed to malaria. One-quarter suffered repeated bouts of amebic dysentery. One-fifth was at risk from schistosomiasis (bilharzia). The tsetse fly threatened 60 million Africans (and their cattle) with trypanosomiasis. Twenty-five million were infected with the AIDS virus. River blindness affected 18 million, of whom over 300,000 were already blind. Rural children were heavily infected with roundworm and hookworm. Chronic diarrhea and respiratory diseases were endemic; epidemics of cholera were commonplace; hepatitis and typhoid were rife. All this was exacerbated by the impact of recurrent flood and drought, famine, collapsing infrastructure, governmental mismanagement, and civil war. What went wrong?

Some believe that Africans are inherently incapable of sustaining viable states without outside help. Such views can be dismissed as racist and plain wrong. After all, there is tribalism in the Balkans and the

Middle East, and corruption almost everywhere. These are the failings of humanity in general, not Africans alone. On the other hand, attributing Africa's plight solely to the way it has been treated by the rest of the world is not totally correct either. Africa was not the world's only victim of external forces. Parts of Asia and Latin America also suffered at the hands of imperialists, but they have nonetheless managed to establish viable states and successful economies.

The difference perhaps is that while other countries recognized the importance of accountability, or making their leaders answerable to the people, African society never paid much regard to this basic concept of democracy. In Africa, a leader was expected to show that he (rarely she) had escaped from ordinary life and was a "Big Man," powerful and rich enough to be a benefactor of the people. Leaders have been expected to use their position for personal gain, and though Africans deplore the fact that their leaders filched billions from the national coffers, criticism is tempered by a fatalistic belief that this is what all leaders do and by the expectation that some of their gains will trickle down to the people.

And the fortitude and tolerance so typical of Africans are not an unalloyed blessing either. On the one hand, they have enabled people to make a living from even the most testing of environmental circumstances. But on the other, they have induced a fatalistic acceptance of the status quo.

"We have a tendency to confuse problems and situations," the foreign minister of Sierra Leone said shortly before his government was overthrown in 1992. "The electricity supply did not deteriorate to its present state overnight; it gradually got worse while we bought candles. There were holes in the roads...that gradually got bigger as we drove around them.... Instead of dealing with the problems, we simply accepted them as situations that we should adapt to."

By the 1990s, though, the men and women who had grown to maturity in independent Africa wanted the continent's problems to be confronted and solved. They were less inclined to blame Africa's woes upon the tyrannies of the past. And attitudes outside Africa changed, too. The end of the Cold War brought an end to unquestioning support for strategically important regimes, such as those in Ethiopia and Zaire. Loans from the World Bank and International Monetary Fund came with tough demands for economic reform, more accountability, democratization, and free elections.

The release of Nelson Mandela from jail on February 11, 1990, was a key moment in these developments. In 1964, he and other leaders of the African National Congress (ANC) had been found guilty of conspiracy to overthrow the South African government and were sentenced to life in prison. But if the apartheid government had expected that locking Mandela away would erase him from the political consciousness

Putswa Tekane has been working in the Carltonville gold mines near Johannesburg since 1980. He lives in a hostel at the mine and goes home to his family in Lesotho at infrequent intervals.

of South Africa, they could hardly have been more wrong. In fact, the stature of Nelson Mandela rose steadily over South Africa and the world. He became the leader, mighty through absence, a prisoner of conscience—silent but forever attached to the truths he had embraced.

Those truths were stated most memorably at his trial. Instead of following the customary procedure of testimony and cross-examination, Mandela had given a full and unambiguous statement of the ANC's political ideals and intentions. He spoke for four hours, concluding with the words:

During my lifetime I have dedicated myself to this struggle of the African people. I have fought against white domination, and I have fought against black domination. I have cherished the ideal of a democratic and free society in which all persons live together in harmony and with equal opportunities. It is an ideal which I hope to live

for and to achieve. But if needs be, it is an ideal for
which I am prepared to die.

Mandela emerged from prison 27 years later, age 71, with the reputation of a saintly hero. Unbowed by the oppression of the white regime, steeled by years of study and contemplation, he had precisely the qualities that the historic moment demanded. He was not a great speaker like Martin Luther King, Jr., nor did he have the artful shrewdness of someone like Mahatma Gandhi. Mandela simply radiated the unflinching, honest authority of an entirely good man. He took command of his own captivity and refused to accept release until his conditions had been met. Most important, he understood that the government's fear of black majority rule could be transformed into fear of an even more terrifying prospect: Without reform, South Africa would collapse into chaos.

By the late 1980s, South Africa was facing bankruptcy. Apartheid had become a preposterous extravagance. Three parliamentary chambers, ten departments of education, health, and welfare (one for each "race" and homeland), plus huge military and state security budgets put an enormous load on the economy. Foreign sanctions and disinvestment increased the strain, while spiraling unemployment, poverty, and civil unrest heightened tension. The conclusion was becoming inescapable. Apartheid would have to go, and with it

white rule. Once the government had recognized this bleak reality, its leaders saw clearly that only a negotiated settlement with Nelson Mandela and the ANC could hope to solve South Africa's mounting economic and social problems.

South Africa's first elections under its new constitution were held in April 1994. The scene at polling stations throughout the country, with millions of voters waiting patiently in lines that wove erratically through the countryside, was one of the most heartening events in modern history. It was the first time that many of the electors had voted, and the first time that an African election had received so much favorable attention from abroad. After so much war and catastrophe, the world stopped to look appreciatively at the face of Africa.

With a black majority government and Nelson Mandela as president, South Africa rejoined the mainstream of African history. The last vestige of white supremacy had been banished from the continent.

Few leaders have generated such universal affection and admiration as Nelson Mandela. Fewer still have relinquished

FOLLOWING PAGES: **The Khomeni San were evicted from their corner of the Kalahari in the 1950s. Since the fall of apartheid, they have won back their rights to the land and are returning, though not to a fully traditional way of life.**

power so soon after achieving it. He had spent more than 50 years fighting for black African rights in South Africa, but he stepped down as president after just 5 years. Unlike many African leaders, he had no wish to take the presidency to his grave. Besides, he had married again, and he wanted to spend time with his grandchildren.

In 1999, Mandela's deputy, 57-year-old Thabo Mbeki, was elected president. Son of an ANC leader who had been convicted and imprisoned with Mandela, he also had devoted his life to the struggle for freedom. After being arrested in southern Rhodesia (now Zimbabwe) on suspicion of terrorist activity, Mbeki was granted political asylum in Tanzania before going to study at the University of Sussex, where he was awarded an M.A. in economics in 1966. For the next ten years he represented the ANC around the world before joining the organization's National Executive.

As the ANC's director of international affairs, Thabo Mbeki played a key role in the negotiations that led to the release of Nelson Mandela and the advent of black majority rule. With those tasks accomplished, Mbeki turned his attention to the problems confronting Africans throughout the continent. "The full meaning of liberation will not be realized until our people are freed both from oppression and from the dehumanizing legacy of deprivation.... I am my brother's keeper; I am my sister's keeper," he pledged in his inaugural speech.

Playing Young Turk to Mandela's elder statesman, Thabo Mbeki called on Africa to rediscover the strengths that made it the birthplace of humanity. He spoke of an African Renaissance that would stir the soul of the continent, reawakening the genius that had inspired the giant obelisks at Aksum, the Egyptian pyramids, the labyrinthine stone walls of Great Zimbabwe, the Benin bronzes, the San rock paintings, ancient Carthage, the universities at Alexandria, Fez and Timbuktu.

Mbeki drew attention to African achievements of the past, but his message was addressed to the post-independence generation and its demand for solutions to the problems of contemporary Africa. He said:

"The call for an African Renaissance is a call to rebellion. We must rebel against the tyrants and the dictators, those who seek to corrupt our societies and steal the wealth that belongs to the people. We must...conduct war against poverty, ignorance and the backwardness of the children. Surely, there must be politicians and business people, youth and women activists, trade unionists, religious leaders, artists and professionals from the Cape to Cairo, from Madagascar to Cape Verde, who are sufficiently enraged by Africa's condition in the world to want to join the mass crusade for Africa's renewal. It is to these that we say, without equivocation, that to be a true African is to be a rebel in the cause of the African Renaissance, whose success in the new

The exaggerated size of the eland in this prehistoric rock painting as compared with the Bushman hunters indicates the importance of the eland to southern Africa's earliest inhabitants.

century and millennium is one of the great historic challenges of our time."

Mbeki's call for an African Renaissance won headlines around the world. Although daunting problems remain, no one should doubt that Africa has the energy, resources, and workforce to become an economic giant of the 21st century. But the prize is more than the wealth and well-being of the continent's people. Africa concerns us all. We hold everything in common—not least our destiny, now that the limits of global exploitation are understood. "The African Renaissance addresses not only the life of the peoples of Africa," says President Mbeki, "it extends the frontiers of human dignity."

W hen South Africa's reviled apartheid regime collapsed and democratic elections brought a black government to power in 1994 with Nelson Mandela as president, a new era of opportunity opened for the victims of racial segregation. But few were as bold as 26-year-old Xoliswa Vanda, who set her sights on becoming the first woman to manage one of South Africa's premier gold mines. Within years, she was the first black woman in the country to hold a blasting certificate and the only woman in a workforce of 5,000 men. Now, if she passes crucial exams, she will be on the company's fast track to management status.

South Africa is the richest nation in Africa, its wealth built upon the enormous reserves of precious minerals. The miners work nearly 2 miles underground, where heat from the Earth's core pushes the temperature to 104° F. Space at the work face is limited and the sound of pneumatic drills deafening. And even here, in one of the world's richest gold mines, the prize they seek is all but invisible. From every ton of ore sent to the surface, a matchhead-size piece of gold is extracted.

Xoliswa is in charge of the explosives used to blast the gold-bearing seam, which may be anything from 1.5 to 8 feet high. She decides where to place charges and how much explosive should be used, and she is legally responsible for the safety of everyone with her.

Xoliswa Vanda (left) is a pioneer—the first black woman to hold a blasting certificate in a South African gold mine. What's more, she's the only woman in a workforce of 5,000. The miners aren't accustomed to taking orders from a woman. But Xoliswa understands their culture very well, she says. "I know how to talk to the men and get them to do exactly what I want. What you mustn't do is take away the dignity of a person."

Chapter 1: SAVANNA

Aiello, L. C., and Wheeler, P., 1995, "The expensive-tissue hypothesis..." *Curr. Anthrop.* 36(2); Alexander, R. M., 1992, "Human locomotion," in: *Cambridge Encycl. of Human Evolution;* Ambrose, S. H., 1984, "The introduction of pastoral adaptations...," in *From Hunters to Farmers;* Baker, B.H., Mohr, P.A. and Williams, L.A.J., 1972, *Geology of the Eastern Rift System of East Africa;* Briggs, J.C., 1987, *Biogeography and Plate Tectonics;* Brown, E. W., 1988, *An Introduction to Solar Energy;* Croze, H., and J. Reader, 2000, *Pyramids of Life;* Harrison, G.A. et al, 1992, *Human Biology;* Houston, D.C., 1979, "The adaptations of scavengers," in: *Serengeti;* Iliffe, J., 1995, *Africans: The History of a Continent;* Leakey, M.D., and J. M. Harris (eds.), 1987, *Laetoli;* Lithgow-Bertelloni, C. and P. G. Silver, 1998, "Dynamic topography..." in *Nature* 395; Lovejoy, C.O., 1981, "The origin of man," *Science* 211; Meadows, M.E., 1996, "Biogeography," in *The Physical Geography of Africa;* Muriuki, G., 1974, *A History of the Kikuyu;* Nance, R. D. et al, 1988, "The supercontinent cycle," *Sci. Am.,* July; Nyamweru, C., 1996, "The African Rift System," in *The Physical Geography of Africa;* Pollitz, F. F., 1999, "From rifting to drifting," *Nature* 398; Reader, J., 1999, *Africa: A Biography of the Continent;* Ross, P.E. 1991, "Hard words," *Sci. Am.* 264(4); Rouhani, S., and S. Jones, 1992, "Bottlenecks in human evolution," in: *Cambridge Encycl. of Human Evolution;* Routledge, W.S. and K., 1910, *With a Prehistoric People;* Schaller, G.B., and G.R. Lowther, 1969, "The relevance of carnivore behavior...," *SW. J. Anthrop.* 25 (pt 4); Sinclair A.R.E., and P. Arcese (eds.), 1995, *Serengeti II;* Steudel, K. L., 1994, "Locomotor energetics and hominid evolution," *Evol. Anthrop.* 3 (pt 2); Summerfield, M. A., 1996, "Tectonics, geology, and long-term landscape development," in *The Physical Geography of Africa;* Tattersall, J., 2000, "Once we were not alone," *Sci. Am.,* January; Van Hoven, W.W., 1991, "Mortality in kudu populations..." *Revue Zoologique Africaine* 105; Wheeler, P.E., 1984, "The evolution of bipedalism...". *J. Hum. Evol.* 13; Wheeler, P.E., 1992, "The thermoregulatory advantages of large body size..." *J. Hum. Evol.* 23; Wilson, A.C. et al., 1987, "Mitochrondrial clans...," in *Human genetics;* Wright, R., 1991, "Quest for the mother tongue," *Atlantic Monthly.*

Chapter 2: DESERT

Attenborough, D., 1984, *The Living Planet;* Baier, S., and P. . Lovejoy, 1977, "The Tuareg of the central Sudan," in *Slavery in Africa;* Beazley, C.R., and E. Prestage (trans. & eds.), 1896, 1899: Azurara, G.E. de. c.1450, *The Chronicle of the Discovery and Conquest of Guinea;* Berger, A., 1988, "Milankovitch and climate," *Rev. Geophys.* 26 (pt.4); Bulliet, R.B., 1975, *The Camel and the Wheel;* Butzer, K., 1976, *Early Hydraulic Civilization in Egypt;* Caton-Thompson, G., 1934, "The camel in dynastic Egypt," *Man* 34:21; Cloudsley-Thompson, J.L. (ed.), 1984, *Sahara Desert.* Clutton-Brock, J., 1993, "The spread of domestic animals in Africa," in *The Archaeology of Africa;* Curtin, P.D., 1984, *Cross-cultural Trade in World History;* Curtin, P.D., 1969, *The Atlantic Slave Trade;* El-Baz, F., 1998, "Aeolian deposits...," *Sahara* 10; Garrard, T.F., 1982, "Myth and metrology," *J. Afr. Hist.* 23; Gowlett, J., 1984, *Ascent to Civilization;* Haaland, R., 1992, "Fish, pots and grain," *Afr. Archaeol. Rev.* 10; Heinzel, H. et al, *The Birds of Britain and Europe;* Hopkins, A.G., 1973, *An Economic History of West Africa;* Iliffe, J., 1995; Imbrie, J., 1982, "Astronomical theory of the Pleistocene Ice Ages," *Icarus* 50; Junge, C.E., 1979, "The importance of mineral dust...," in *Saharan Dust;* Kassas, M., and K. H. Batanouny, 1984, "Plant ecology," in *Sahara Desert;* Keenan, J., 1977, *The Tuareg;* Keenan, J., 2000, "The father's friend," *Anthrop. Today* 16(4); Lamprey, H.F. 1988, "Report on the desert encroachment..." (UNESCO/UNEP) [*Desertification* Control Bull. 17, 1.]; Lancaster, N., 1996, "Desert Environments," in *The Physical Geography of Africa;* Levtzion, N., and J. F. P. Hopkins, 1981, *Corpus of Early Arabic Sources for West African History;* Lhote, H., 1987, "Oasis of art in the Sahara," *Nat. Geog.,* August; Lovejoy, P.E.,1986, *Salt of the Desert Sun;* Markham, C.R. (ed.), 1878, *John Hawkins;* McCauley, J.F., et al, 1986, "Palaeodrainages of the Eastern Sahara" *IEEE Trans. Geosci. Remote Sens.* GE-24 (pt.4); McGinnies, W. et al, 1968, *Deserts of the World;* Moreau, R.E., 1972, *The Palearctic-African Bird Migration Systems;* Multhauf, R.P., 1978, *Neptune's Gift;* Nachtigal, G., 1980, *Sahara and Sudan,* vol. 2; Nicklung W.G., and J. A. Gillies, 1993, "Dust emissions and transport...," *Sedimentology* 40(5); Nicolaisen, J., 1963, *Ecology and Culture of the Pastoral Tuareg,* National Museum of Copenhagen; O'Connor, D., 1993, "Urbanism in bronze age Egypt and northeast Africa," in *The Archaeology of Africa;* Oliver, R., 1991, *The African Experience;* Pettet, A., 1986, "Migratory birds," in *Sahara Desert;* Polis, Gary A. (ed.) 1991, *The Ecology of Desert Communities;* Pratt, D.J., and M. D. Gwynne, 1977, *Rangeland Management and Ecology in East Africa;* Prospero, J.M., R. A. Glaccum, and R. T. Nees, 1981, "Atmospheric transport of soil dust...," *Nature* 289; Reader, J., 1999; Roset, J.P., 1987, "Palaeoclimatic and cultural conditions of neolithic development..." in *Prehistory of Arid North Africa;* Rowley-Conwy, P., 1988, "The camel in the Nile valley," *Archaeol.* 74; Said, R., 1993, *The River Nile;* Said, R., 1997, "The role of the desert...," *Sahara* 9:20; Saunders, A.C. de C.M., 1982, *A Social History of the Black Slaves and Freemen in Portugal 1441-1555;* Shaw, T. et al (eds.), 1993, *The Archaeology of Africa;* Smith, A.B.1992, *Pastoralism in Africa;* Smith, G., 1984, "Climate," in *Sahara Desert;* Stemler, A., 1984, "The transition from food collecting...," in *From Hunters to Farmers;* Sultan, M., et al, 1999, "Monitoring the urbanization of the Nile Delta, Egypt," *Ambio* 28 (7); Swain, A., 1997, "Ethiopia, Sudan, and Egypt," *J. Mod. Afr. Stu.* 35 (4); *The Times Atlas* 1985; Theroux, P., 1997, "The imperilled Nile Delta," *Nat. Geog.,* January; Tucker, C.J., H. E. Dregne, and W. W. Newcomb, 1991, "Expansion and contraction of the Sahara Desert...," *Science* 253; Tucker, C.J., and S.E. Nicholson, 1999, "Variations in the size of the Sahara Desert from 1980 to 1997," *Ambio* 28 (7); Vines, G., 1992, "Winning streak for sheiks," *New Sci.* 136; Wickens, G.E. 1984, "Flora," in *Sahara Desert;* Willert, D.J. von, et al. 1992, *Life Strategies of Succulents in Deserts;* World Resources Institute, *World Resources 1998-99: A Guide to the Global Environment.*

Chapter 3: RAIN FOREST

Akobundu, I.O., 1991, "Weeds in human affairs...," *Weed Technol.* 5; Bailey, R.C., and T.N. Headland, 1991, "The tropical rain forest," *Hum Ecol.* 19 (2); Boyce, N., 2000, "Blocking malaria," *New Sci.,* 8 July; Breasted, J.H., 1906-7, *Ancient Records of Egypt.* 5 vols.; Campbell, B., 1983, *Human Ecology;* CLIMAP Project Members, 1976, "The surface of the ice-age Earth," *Science* 191; Connah, G., 1987, *African Civilizations;* Deacon, J. 1990, "Changes in the archaeological record in South Africa...," in *The World at 18000 BP,* vol. 2; Dobson, A., 1993, "People and disease," in *Cambridge Encycl. of Human Evolution;* Fairhead, J., and M. Leach, 1996, *Misreading the African Landscape;* Fairhead, J., and M. Leach, 1998, *Reframing Deforestation;* Flenley, J.R., 1979, *The Equatorial Rain Forest;* Fuller, F., 1921 (1967), *A Vanished Dynasty: Ashanti;* Gowlett, J., 1984, *Ascent to Civilization;* Grainger, A., 1996, "Forest environments," in *The Physical Geography of Africa;* Hamilton, A., 1976, "Significance of patterns of distribution...," *Palaeoecol. Afr.* 9; Harlan, J.R., 1976, *Crops and Man;* Harrison, G.A., H. J. M.Tanner, D. R. Pilbeam, and P. T. Baker, 1992, *Human Biology;* Hodgkin, T. 1975, *Nigerian Perspectives;* Hopkins, A.G., 1973, *An Economic History of West Africa;* Iliffe, J., 1995; Kingdon, J., 1989; Livingstone, F.B., 1958, "Anthropological implications of sickle cell gene...," *Am. Anthrop.* 60; Mattingly, P.F., 1983, "The palaeogeography of mosquito-borne disease," *Biol. J. Linn. Soc.* 199; Mayr, E., and R. J. O'Hara, 1986, "The biogeographical evidence supporting the Pleistocene refuge hypothesis," *Evolution* 40; Meadows, M.E., 1996, "Biogeography," in *The Physical Geography of Africa;* Miracle, M.P., 1965, "The introduction and spread of maize in Africa," *J. Afr. Hist.* 6; Mitchell, P., 1990, in *The World at 18000 BP, vol. 2;* Myers, N., 1996, "Biodiversity and biodepletion," in *The Physical Geography of Africa;* Ndoye, O., and D. Kaimowitz, 2000, "Macro-economics, markets and the humid forests of Cameroon...," *Journal of Modern African Studies,* 38 (2); Nisbet, E., 1991, *Living Earth;* Pearce, F., 1997, "Lost forests leave West Africa dry," *New Sci.,* 18 October; Pearce, F., 2000, "Malariasphere," *New Sci.,* 15 July; Phillips, P., 1992, "Banking on it," *Weekend Guardian,* 3 October; Richards, P.W., 1993, "Africa the 'Odd Man Out,'" in *Tropical Forest Ecosystems in Africa and South America;* Roberts, N., 1992, "Climatic change in the past," in *Cambridge Encycl. of Human Evolution;* Roth, H.L., 1903, *Great Benin;* Schebesta, P., 1933, *Among Congo Pigmies;* Tewolde, Berhan, 1992, "Amani forest [Tanzania] study," cited in *The Environmental Problems of Northern Ethiopia;* Van Zinderen Bakker, E.M., 1982, "African palaeoenvironments...," *Palaeoecol. Afr.* 15; Vansina, J., 1990, *Paths in the Rainforest;* Whitmore, T.C., 1998, *An Introduction to Tropical Rain Forests;* Wilks, I. (ed.), 1993, *Forests of Gold;* Wilks, I., 1975, *Asante in the Nineteenth Century;* World Health Organization, 2001, "Malaria statistics from WHO Fact Sheet," No 94, October 1998. World Resources Institute, 1998, *World Resources 1998-1999: A Guide to the Global Environment.*

Chapter 4: MOUNTAINS

Baker, B.H., P. A. Mohr, and L. A. J. Williams, 1972, *Geology of the Eastern Rift System of Africa.;* Barker, B.J., 1989, *Dias and Da Gama;* Brandt, S.A., 1984, "New perspectives on the origins of food production...," in *From Hunters to Farmers;* Butzer, K.W., 1981, "Rise and fall of Axum, Ethiopia," *Am. Antiq.,* 46 (3); Buxton, B.R., 1970, *The Abyssinians;* Casson, L., 1989, *The Periplus Maris Erythraei;* Connah, G., 1987, *African Civilizations;* Contenson, H. de, 1981, "Pre-Aksumite culture, vol. I," in UNESCO, *General History of Africa;* Crawford, O.G.S., 1958, *Ethiopian Itineraries, c1400-1524;* De Waal, A., 1997, *Famine Crimes, Politics and the Disaster Relief Industry in Africa;* Demissew, S., 1988, "The floristic composition of the Menagesha State Forest..." *Mount. Res. Devel.* 8; Ermias, B., 1986, "Landuse planning...," *SINET Ethiop. J. Sci.* 9 (suppl.); Eshetu, Z., and P. Hgberg, 2000, "Reconstruction of forest site history...," *Ambio* 29; Fattovich, R., 1990, "Remarks on the Pre-Axumite period...," *J. Ethiop. Stud.* 23; Jones, G., 1988, "Endemic crop plants of Ethiopia," *Walia* 11; Kingdon, J., 1989, *Island Africa:* Kobish(ch)anov, Y.M., 1981, "Aksum," in UNESCO, 1981-93, *General History of Africa;* Kobishchanov, Y.M. (trans. L.T. Kapitanoff), 1979, *Axum;* Korn, D.A., 1986, *Ethiopia, the United States* and the Soviet Union; **Lefort, R.**, 1983, *Ethiopia: An Heretical Revolution?*; **Munro-Hay, S.**, 1991, *An African Civilisation*; **Phillipson, D.W.**, 1994, Aksum (unpub. summary MS); **Pohjonen, V., and T. Pukkala**, 1990, "*Eucalyptus globulus* in Ethiopian forestry," *For. Ecol. Mgmt.* 36; **Rodgers, A.**, 1992, "Ethiopia," in *The Conservation Atlas of Tropical Forests: Africa*; **Sauer, C.O.**, 1952, *Agricultural Origins and Dispersals*; **Seaman, J. and J. Holt**, 1975, "The Ethiopian famine of 1973-4," *Proceedings of the Nutritional Society* 34; **Simoons, F.J.**, 1965, "Some questions on the economic prehistory of Ethiopia," *J. Afr. Hist.* 6; **Summerfield, M.A.**, 1996, "Tectonics, geology and long-term landscape development," in *The Physical Geography of Africa*; **Tamrat, T.**, 1972, *Church and State in Ethiopia*; **Taylor, D.**, 1996, "Mountains," in *The Physical Geography of Africa*; **Turnbull et al**, 1988, "Volume production...," *Appita* 41; **Williams, J.E., and I. H. Booker** (eds.), 1997, *Eucalypt ecology*; **Yalden, D.W.**, 1983, "The extent of the high ground in Ethiopia...," *SINET, Ethiop. J. Sci.* 6(1).

Chapter 5: SAHEL

Classon, A.T., 1980, "The animal remains from Tell es Sinn...," *Anatolica* 7; **Clutton-Brock, J.**, 1992, "Domestication of animals," in *Cambridge Encycl. of Human Evolution*; **Clutton-Brock, J.**, 1993, "The spread of domestic animals in Africa," in *The Archaeology of Africa*; **Cook, G.C., and S. K. Kajubi**, 1966, "Tribal incidence of lactase deficiency...," *The Lancet*, 2 April; **Ellis, W.E.**, 1987, "Africa's Sahel," *Nat. Geog.*, August; **Gerster, G.**, 1986, "Tsetse, fly of the deadly sleep," *Nat. Geog.*, December; **Giblin, J.**, 1990, "Trypanosomiasis control...," *J. Afr. Hist.* 31; **Grigson, C.**, 1980, "Size and sex," in *The Beginnings of Agriculture*; **Johnson, R.C. et al**, 1981, "Genetic interpretation of racial and ethnic differences...," *Hum. Biol.* 53; **Kay, R.N.B.**, 1997, "Responses of African livestock...," *J. Arid Environments* 37 (4); **Kretchmer, N.**, 1972, "Lactose and lactase," *Sci. Am.* 227 (4); **Leak, S.G.A.**, 1999, *Tsetse Biology and Ecology*; **Lowe-McConnell, R.H.**, 1984, "The biology of the river systems...," in *The Niger and Its Neighbours*; **MacFarlane, W.V.** et al, 1971, "Hierarchy of water...," *Nature* 234; **McCracken, R.D.**, 1971, "Lactose deficiency," *Curr. Anthrop.* 12; **McIntosh, R.J. and S.K.**, 1984, "Early Iron Age economy...," in *From Hunters to Farmers*; **McIntosh, R.J.**, 1992, "Historical view of the semiarid tropics," paper presented at the 1992 Carter Lecture Series, Univ. of Florida; **McIntosh, S.K. and R.J.**, 1993, "Cities without citadels," in *The Archaeology of Africa*; **McIntosh, S.K. and R.J.**, 1980, "Prehistorical investigations...," *Brit. Archaeol. Reps*; **McNaughton, S.J.**, 1979, "Grazing as an optimization process," *Am. Nat.* 113; **Meadows, M.E.**, 1996, "Biogeography," in *The Physical Geography of Africa*; **Nash, T. A. M.**, 1969, *Africa's Bane*; **Pearce, Fred**, 2000, "Inventing Africa," *New Sci.*, 12 August; **Riesman, P.**, 1984, "The Fulani in a development context," in *Life Before the Drought*; **Schmidt-Nielsen, K.**, 1964, *Desert Animals*; **Simoons, F.J.**, 1973, "The determinants of dairying...," *Ecol. Food Nutr.* 2; **Smith, A.B.**, 1992, *Pastoralism in Africa*; **Spencer, P.**, 1968, *The Samburu*; **Waller, R.D.**, 1990, "Tsetse fly in western Narok, Kenya," *J. Afr. Hist.* 31; **Wendorf, F.D., and R. Schild**, 1995, "Are the early Holocene cattle in the eastern Sahara domestic or wild?" *Evol. Anthrop.* 3(4); **Wendorf, F., and R. Schild**, 1984, "The emergence of food production...," in *From Hunters to Farmers*; **World Resources Institute**, 1998, *World Resources 1998-99: A Guide to the Global Environment*; **Zimmer, C.**, 1998, "A sleeping storm," *Discover*, August.

Chapter 6: GREAT LAKES

Adams, W.M., 1996, "Lakes," in *The Physical Geography of Africa*; **African Rights**, 1995, *Rwanda: Death, despair and defiance*; **Argyle, W.J.**, 1971, "A critique of one rural-urban dichotomy," Unpublished MS, quoted in *Natal/KwaZulu*; **Balihuta, A.M.**, 1999, "Education provision and outcome...," *Uganda Journal* 45 (August); **Berger, A.**, 1988, "Milankovitch and climate," *Rev. Geophys.* 26 (pt 4); **Croze, H., and J. Reader**, 2000, *Pyramids of Life*; **Cohen, J.**, 2000, "The hunt for the origin of AIDS," *Atlantic Monthly*, October; **Cotton, A.**, 2000, "Sex and education," *The Guardian*, 7 July; **De Langhe, E., R. et al**, 1996, "Plantain in the early Bantu world," in *The growth of farming communities in Africa...*; **De Waal, A.**, 1994, "Genocide in Rwanda," *Anthrop. Today* 10(3); **Essex, M.**, 1999, "The new AIDS epidemic," *Harvard Magazine*, Sept-Oct 1999; **Fryer, G.**, 1997, "Biological implications of a Late Pleistocene desiccation...," *Hydrobiologia* 354; **Gibbon, P.**, 1997, *Of saviours and punks*, CDR Working Paper 97.3; **Harris, C.K. et al**, 1995, "Socio-economic impacts of introduced species...," in *The Impact of Species Changes in African Lakes*; **Iliffe, J.**, 1979, *A Modern History of Tanganyika*; **Imbrie, J.**, 1982, "Astronomical theory of the Pleistocene Ice Ages," *Icarus* 50; **International Food Policy Research Institute** (IFPRI), 1991, *Facts and Figures: International Agricultural Research*; **Johnson, T.C. et al**, 1996, "Late Pleistocene desiccation of Lake Victoria...," *Science* 273; **Johnson, T.C. et al**, 2000, "The Holocene history of Lake Victoria," *Ambio* 29, No. 1; **Kasoki, A.B.K.**, 1999, "Regional inequality in Uganda...," *The Uganda Journal* 45 (August); **Kingdon, J.**, 1989; **Louis, W.R.**, 1963, *Ruanda-Urundi 1884-1919*; **Lowe-McConnell R.H.**, 1987, *Ecological Studies in Tropical Fish Communities*; **Morris, M.** (Head of Development Studies, Univ. of Natal), 25 Sept. 2000; **Ochumba, P.B.O.**, 1995, "Limnological changes in Lake Victoria...," in *The Impact of Species Changes in African Lakes*; **Oliver, R.**, 1991, *The African Experience*; **Prunier, G.**, 1995, *The Rwanda Crisis 1959-1994*; **Reynolds, J.E., et al**, 1995, "Thirty years on," in *The Impact of Species Changes in African Lakes*; **Roberts, A.D.** (ed.) 1990, *The Colonial Moment in Africa*; **Stiassny, M.L.J., and A. Meyer**, 1999, "Cichlids of the Rift lakes," *Sci. Am.*, February; **Sutton, J.E.G.**, 1990, *A Thousand Years of East Africa*; **Sutton, J.E.G.**, 1993, "The antecedents of the interlacustrine kingdoms," *J. Afr. Hist.* 34; **Vail, L.** (ed.), 1989, *The Creation of Tribalism in Southern Africa*; **World Resources Institute**, 1998, *World Resources 1998-99: A Guide to the Global Environment*; **Wrigley, C.**, 1989, "Bananas in Buganda," *Azania* 24.

Chapter 7: COAST

Attenborough, D., 1984; **Axelson, E.**, 1949/1969, *South-east Africa 1488-1530*; **Bakari, R. and J. Andersson**, 1998, "Economic liberalization and its effect...," *Ambio* 27, no. 8; **Casson, L.**, 1989, *The Periplus Maris Erythraei*; **Connah, G.**, 1987, *African Civilizations*; **Connell, J.**, 1978, "Diversity in tropical rainforests and coral reefs," *Science* 199; **Crowder, M.**, 1985, "The First World War and its consequences," in UNESCO, *General History of Africa*, vol. 7; **Eltis, D.**, 1990, "The volume, age/sex ratios, and African impact...," *J. Afr. Hist.* 31; **Eltis, D.**, 1987, *Economic Growth and the Ending of the Transatlantic Slave Trade*; **Freeman-Grenville, G.S.P.**, 1975, *The East African Coast*; **Gann, L.H.**, 1975, "Economic development in Germany's African empire...," in *Colonialism in Africa*, vol. 4; **Hodges, G.W.T.**, 1978, "African manpower statistics...," *J. Afr. Hist.* 19; **Iliffe, John**, 1995, *Africans*; **Inikori, J.E.**, 1977, "The import of firearms...," *J. Afr. Hist.* 28; **Johannes, R.E.**, 1975, "Pollution and degradation...," in *Tropical Marine Pollution*; **Johnstone, R.W. et al**, 1998, "The status of the coral reefs...," *Ambio* 27, no. 8; **Kingdon, J.**, 1989; **Lovejoy, Paul E.**, 1989, "The impact of the Atlantic slave trade...," *J. Afr. Hist.* 30; **Lovejoy, P.**, 1983, *Transformations in Slavery*; **Lowe-McConnell, R.H.**, 1987, *Ecological Studies in Tropical Fish Communities*; **Manning, P.**, 1990, *Slavery and African Life*; **Metcalf, G.**, 1987, "A microcosm of why African sold slaves," *J. Afr. Hist.* 28; **Miller, J.C.**, 1988, *Way of Death*; **Omar, N.S.**, 1997, *Zanzibar Clove Industry*, Zanzibar State Trading Corporation website; **Orme, A.R.**, 1996, "Coastal environments," in *The Physical Geography of Africa*; **Reader, J.**, 1999; **Richard, W.A.**, 1980, "The import of firearms...," *J. Afr. Hist.* 2; **Snow, P.**, 1988, *The Star Raft*; **Sorokin, Y.I.**, 1995, *Coral Reef Ecology*; **Sutton, J.E.G.** (ed.), 1996, "The growth of farming communities...," *Azania* 29-30; **Wilkinson, C. et al**, 1999, "Ecological and socioeconomic impacts...," *Ambio* 28, no. 2; **World Resources Institute**, 1998, *World Resources 1998-99: A Guide to the Global Environment*; "Zanzibar's seaweed farming," 1995, *Ambio* 24 (December).

Chapter 8: SOUTHERN AFRICA

"Africa: The heart of the matter. 2000," *The Economist*, 13 May. 24; **Allen, H.D.**, 1996, "Mediterranean environments," in *The Physical Geography of Africa*; **Bangura, P.**, 1991, Interview on 7 October 1991; **Boyd, F.R., and J. J. Gurney**, 1986, "Diamonds and the African lithosphere," *Science* 232; **Cocks, L.M.R.** (ed.), 1981, *The Evolving Earth*; **Cowling , R.M. et al**, 1992, "Concepts and patterns of endemism...," in *The Ecology of the Fynbos*; **Deacon, H.J.**, 1989, "Late Pleistocene palaeoecology and archaeology...," in *The Human Revolution*; **Deacon, J.**, 1999, "South African rock art," *Evol. Anthrop.* 8 (2); **Denny, C.**, 2000, "Uganda losing its lustre...," *The Guardian*, 21 July; **Dumbuya, A.R.**, 1991, Voice of America interview, 5 October 1991; **Elphick, R. and H. Giliomee** (eds.), 1989, *The Shaping of South African Society, 1652-1840*; **Geological Society of South Africa**, *Some Superlatives of Geology in South Africa*; **Hunter, D.R., and P. J. Hamilton**, 1978, "The Bushveld complex," in *Evolution of the Earth's Crust*; **Iliffe, J.**, 1995; **Jefferson, T.**, 1782, *Notes on Virginia*, quoted in *Back to Africa*; **Lee, R.B.**, 1969, "Eating Christmas...," *Natural History*, 14-22 December; **Lee, R.B.**, 1968, "What hunters do for a living...," in *Man the Hunter*; **Levinson, O.**, *Diamonds in the Desert*; **Mbeki, T.**, 1998, "The African Renaissance Statement," 13 August 1998; **Morgan, l.**, 1964, *Ancient Society*, quoted in *Land Filled with Flies*; **Nisbet, E.G.**, 1991, *Living Earth*; **Platteau, J.-P.**, 1990-1, "The food crisis in Africa, vol. II," in *The Political Economy of Hunger*; **Robertson, M.**, 1974, *Diamond fever*; **Shillington, K.**, 1989, *History of Africa*; **Swarns, R.L.**, 2000, "Gaborone Journal," *New York Times*, 6 October. A4; **Thompson, L.**, 1990, *A History of South Africa*; **Transparency International**, 2000, "Zimbabwe: the most travelled African leader," *Corruption Reports*, April 2000; **Traill, A.**, 1978, "The languages of the Bushmen," in *The Bushmen*; **Turrell, R.V.**, 1982, "Kimberley: labour and compounds...," in *Industrialization and Social Change in South Africa*; **Turrell, R.V.**, 1984, "Kimberley's model compounds...," *J. Afr. Hist.* 25; **Turrell, R.V.**, 1987, *Capital and Labour of the Kimberley Diamond Fields, 1871-1890*; **Van der Horst, S.**, 1942, *Native Labour in South Africa*; **Worger, W.H.**, 1987, *South Africa's City of Diamonds*.

about the author

John Reader is the acclaimed author of *Africa: A Biography of the Continent*, which was hailed as "awe-inspiring" and "breathtaking in scope and detail." He has lived and traveled in Africa for many years. Most recently, he wrote and consulted for the PBS production *Africa*.

acknowledgments

First I want to thank the scientists, historians, commentators, authors and interviewees for the information that forms the basis of my narrative. Published sources are acknowledged in a comprehensive chapter by chapter bibliography, but that is hardly an adequate expression of gratitude for all the help and hospitality I have received during the years I have worked in Africa. I offer my deepest thanks to all, and of course take full responsibilty for any errors or misinterpretation. The publication of my *Africa: A Biography of the Continent* in 1997/8 coincided with planning for the NGS/PBS television series on Africa. As consultant to the series I also undertook to write a companion volume—all of which leaves me indebted to Jeremy Bradshaw and Andrew Jackson, Chris Weber, Fred Kaufmann, Jennifer Lawson and Kevin Mulroy. My thanks to all. The task of writing the companion volume was eased considerably by an Ella Walker Fellowship from the Rockefeller Foundation. My thanks are due to the Foundation—to Lincoln Chen and Susan Garfield in New York, and most especially to Gianna Celli and the staff of the Villa Serbelloni in Bellagio. In many ways, this book is an extension of *Africa: A Biography of the Continent*. But the structure is completely different. Where the *Biography* took an in-depth chronological approach, *Africa* examines the subject from a more directly environmental point of view. Thus the books are complementary—neither replaces the other—but this is wholly National Geographic's book. On the companion volume the involvement of Kevin Mulroy, Johnna Rizzo, Greta Arnold, Michael Lewis and John Paine was invaluable, while my work on this edition has been most ably co-ordinated by Barbara Brownell Grogan and Lauren Pruneski—my thanks to all.

But nothing gets built without a sound foundation, and on this score I am profoundly grateful to Brigitte and our daughter Alice for the love and constancy that make life—and work—a joy.

illustrations credits

index

africa

JOHN READER

Published by the National Geographic Society

John M. Fahey, Jr., *President and Chief Executive Officer*
Gilbert M. Grosvenor, *Chairman of the Board*
Nina D. Hoffman, *Executive Vice President;*
  President, Book Publishing Group

Prepared by the Book Division

Kevin Mulroy, *Senior Vice President and Publisher*
Leah Bendavid-Val, *Director of Photography Publishing*
  and Illustrations
Marianne R. Koszorus, *Director of Design*

Barbara Brownell Grogan, *Executive Editor*
Elizabeth Newhouse, *Director of Travel Publishing*
Carl Mehler, *Director of Maps*

Staff for this edition

Lauren Pruneski, *Project Editor*
Jane Menyawi, *Illustrations Editor*
Cinda Rose, *Art Director*
Sanaa Akkach, *Designer*
Rick Wain, *Production Project Manager*
Robert Waymouth, *Illustrations Specialist*

Jennifer A. Thornton, *Managing Editor*
Gary Colbert, *Production Director*

Staff for previous edition

Kevin Mulroy, *Editor*
John Paine, *Text Editor*
Greta Arnold, *Illustrations Editor*
Johnna Rizzo, *Assistant Editor*
Anne Withers, *Researcher*
Melissa Farris, *Design Assistant*
Carol B. Lutyk, *Contributing Editor*
Cynthia Combs, *Illustrations Assistant*

Manufacturing and Quality Management

Christopher A. Liedel, *Chief Financial Officer*
Phillip L. Schlosser, *Vice President*
John T. Dunn, *Technical Director*
Chris Brown, *Director*
Maryclare Tracy, *Manager*
Nicole Elliott, *Manager*

Founded in 1888, the National Geographic Society is one of the largest nonprofit scientific and educational organizations in the world. It reaches more than 285 million people worldwide each month through its official journal, NATIONAL GEOGRAPHIC, and its four other magazines; the National Geographic Channel; television documentaries; radio programs; films; books; videos and DVDs; maps; and interactive media. National Geographic has funded more than 8,000 scientific research projects and supports an education program combating geographic illiteracy.

For more information, please call
1-800-NGS LINE (647-5463)
or write to the following address:

National Geographic Society
1145 17th Street N.W.
Washington, D.C. 20036-4688 U.S.A.

Visit us online at www.nationalgeographic.com

For information about special discounts
for bulk purchases, please contact
National Geographic Books Special Sales:
ngspecsales@ngs.org

Library of Congress Cataloging-in-Publication Data
Reader, John.
  Africa / by John Reader. -- [Rev. ed.].
    p. cm.
  Includes bibliographical references and index.
  ISBN 978-1-4262-0203-2 (deluxe) -- ISBN 978-1-4262-0202-5 (regular)
  1. Africa--Geography. 2. Africa--Pictorial works. I. Title.
DT6.7.R43 2007
960--dc22
                                    2007007903

ISBN: 978-1-4262-0202-5 (regular)
ISBN 978-1-4262-0203-2 (deluxe)
Printed in U.S.A.